毕淑敏
双语美文

A Bilingual Edition of
Beautiful Stories
by Bi Shumin

U0725844

温暖世间的灯

The Glow in Our Winter

毕淑敏 著

朱虹 刘海明 译

GUANGXI NORMAL UNIVERSITY PRESS

广西师范大学出版社

·桂林·

温暖世间的灯
WENNUAN SHIJIAN DE DENG

出版统筹：张俊显
品牌总监：耿　磊
选题策划：耿　磊
责任编辑：王芝楠
助理编辑：韩杰文
美术编辑：卜翠红　刘冬敏
营销编辑：杜文心　钟小文
责任技编：李春林

图书在版编目（CIP）数据

温暖世间的灯：汉、英 / 毕淑敏著；朱虹，刘海明
译 . 一桂林：广西师范大学出版社，2020.1
（毕淑敏双语美文）
ISBN 978-7-5598-2401-1

Ⅰ . ①温… Ⅱ . ①毕…②朱…③刘… Ⅲ . ①散文集一
中国一当代一汉、英 Ⅳ . ①I267

中国版本图书馆 CIP 数据核字（2019）第 273113 号

广西师范大学出版社出版发行

（广西桂林市五里店路 9 号　邮政编码：541004）
　网址：http://www.bbtpress.com
出版人：黄轩庄
全国新华书店经销
保定市中画美凯印刷有限公司印刷
（保定市西三环 1566 号　邮政编码：071000）
开本：880 mm × 1 350 mm　1/32
印张：6　　字数：120 千字
2020 年 1 月第 1 版　　2020 年 1 月第 1 次印刷
印数：0 001~6 000 册　　定价：39.80 元

如发现印装质量问题，影响阅读，请与出版社发行部门联系调换。

在书中温暖相遇

几年前，广西师范大学出版社出版了我的一套书。在这套书里，我写了自己在遥远西藏的往事，写了当医生的难忘经历，写了担当心理医生时听到的故事和引发的思考……

书是缔造心灵的塑形工具。东方文化中，心并不单单指那个解剖学上的泵血器官，而是汇聚每个人的品格情操的智慧之海。有一颗仁慈之心，会爱世界爱他人爱生活，爱自身也爱大家。有一颗自强之心，会勤学苦练百折不挠，宠辱不惊大智若愚。有一颗尊严之心，会珍惜自然善待万物。有一颗流量充沛羽翼丰满的心，会乘上幻想飞船，抚摸众星的翅膀。

我遇到了朱虹老师，她就是拥有这样一颗多彩之心的睿智长者。很高兴她喜欢我书中的文字。

最初，朱虹老师想挑一些篇章翻译，作为礼物送给远在大洋彼岸的孙女外孙女们珍藏。广西师大出版社的编辑获悉这个想法，郑重邀请朱虹和刘海明老师，将本套书全部翻译出来。

这不是轻易可完成之事，是颇为繁复艰辛的工程。朱虹老师已年近90，是中国社科院德高望重的英美文学研究专家，也是一位把我国很多当代文学作品翻译介绍到国外的杰出翻译家。长期生活在国外的刘海明老师造诣高超文采斐然，和朱虹老师相得益彰珠联璧合。两位老师以醇厚学养和丰富经验，深思熟虑地将这些文字，按照英语思维方式和阅读风格，给予精彩转化，赋予它们以另外一种语言表达的鲜活生命。

补充一个小插曲。我的散文"精神的三间小屋"，被选入2018年教育部审定的全国义务教育语文教科书九年级上册。刘海明老师加班加点，将这篇文章翻译出来，收入本套书，真是雪中送炭。

面对这套双语书，我心中充盈知遇之恩和感念之情，在此向所有付出心血的老师们深表谢意！

人生是砥砺向前且充满顿挫的历程，不时筋疲力尽茫然四顾。这本小书的故事和它的成书过程，让我又一次相信，行程中有不期而至的风雨，更有美好温暖的巧遇。朱虹、海明老师和我在文字中结识，现在，我期待着——我们和你——亲爱的读者，在书中相逢。

之后，让咱们再次充满信心地出发！

2019年11月5日

When We Meet Inside a Book

A few years ago, Guangxi Normal University Press published a collection of my stories. In them, I wrote about the years I spent in remote Tibet, my unforgettable experience working as a physician, and stories and musings I gathered as a counseling psychologist.

Works of literature help shape our heart. In Eastern cultures, the heart is the sea of wisdom that nurtures our character, other than a mere organ anatomically responsible for pumping blood through the body. It is with the kind heart that one loves the world, others and life; love of oneself and all people. It is with the hardy, aspiring heart that one strives on, never giving up, and is wise, artless and unflappable. It is with the dignified heart that one cherishes nature and is kind to all creatures great and small. It is with the heart brimful of confidence that one floats on wings of imagination, touching the stars.

Then I met Zhu Hong, an erudite elder with such an unfailingly rich heart, and was most delighted that she liked the stories of this collection.

Initially, Zhu Hong had planned to translate a selection of them as a gift to be held dear by her granddaughters across the ocean. However, when the editorial staff of Guangxi Normal University Press learned about this, they decided to invite Zhu Hong and Liu Haiming to translate the entire collection into English.

It was no small undertaking, a project requiring much dedication. Zhu Hong, in her late eighties, is a venerated scholar in the field of English and American Literature with the Chinese Academy of Social Sciences. She is also noted for her incomparable translations of outstanding works of modern Chinese literature, bringing them to a wider international audience. Liu Haiming, an accomplished translator having studied and worked extensively abroad, collaborated with Zhu Hong on this project. The two scholar-translators pored over the Chinese texts and managed to bring out the spirit of the original, and give life to the stories in the English language in all its beauty and flexibility.

Incidentally, my essay "Three Little 'Rooms' for Your Soul" was selected for the 2018 edition of the Ministry of Education-approved high school textbook for Chinese Language and Literature, for the first semester of the ninth year of National Compulsory Education. Beavering away, Liu Haiming had it timely translated for inclusion in the present collection.

As this bilingual collection was ready for printing, I felt most grateful for our privileged connection. My thanks go to all who have put all the hard work into its publication.

Life is a journey, with inevitable challenges and setbacks, which, at times, can wear you out, and loneliness captures you. Yet, for all the storms out of the blue, there are also fortuitous, heartening encounters along the way—a belief borne out by the stories in this collection and its publication. Zhu Hong, Haiming and I met in the pages of these stories, and now I look forward to our encounter with you, dear readers, in this little collection.

Then, brimful of confidence again, we will journey on!

Bi Shumin, November 5, 2019

contents
目 录

contents
目 录

心是一只美丽的小箱子

小时候上学，很惊奇以"心"为偏旁的字怎么那么多？比如：念、想、意、忘、慈、感、愁、思、恶、慰、慧……哈！一个庞大的家族。

除了这些安然地卧在底下的"心"以外，还有更多迫不及待站着的"心"。这就是那些带"竖心"旁的字，比如：忆、怀、快、怕、怪、恼、恨、惭、悄、惯、惜……原谅我就此打住，因为再举下去，实在有卖弄学问和抄字典的嫌疑。

从这些例证，可以想见当年老祖宗造字的时候，是多么重视"心"的作用，横着用了一番还嫌不过瘾，又把它立起来，再用一遭。

其实，从医学解剖的观点来看，心虽然极其重要，但它的主要工作，是负责把血液输送到人的全身，好像一台水泵，干的是机械方面的活儿，并不主管思维。汉字里把那么多情绪和智慧的感受，都堆到它身上，有点张冠李戴。

真正统率我们思想的，是大脑。

人脑是一个很奇妙的器官。比如学者用"脑海"来描述它，就很有意思。一个脑壳才有多大？假若把它比成一个陶罐，至多装上三四个可乐瓶子的水，也就满满当当了。如果是儿童，容量更有限，没准儿刚倒光几个易拉罐，就沿着罐口溢出水来了。可是，不管是成人还是小孩的大脑，人们都把它形容成个"海"，一个能容纳百川波涛汹涌的大海。这是为什么？

大脑是我们情感和智慧的大本营，它主宰着我们的思维和决策。它能记住许多东西，也能忘了许多东西。记住什么忘却什么，并不完全听从意志的指挥。比方明天老师要检查背诵默写一篇课文，你反复念了好多遍，就是记不住。就算好不容易记住了，到了课堂上一紧张，得，又忘得差不多了。你就是急得面红耳赤抓耳挠腮，也毫无办法。若是几个月后再问你，那更是云山雾罩一塌糊涂。可有些当时只是无意间看到听到的事情，比如路旁老奶奶一句夸奖的话，秋天庭院里一片飘落的叶子，当时的印象很清淡，却不知被谁施了魔法，能像刀刻斧劈一般，永远留在我们记忆的年轮上。

我不知道科学家最近研究出了哪些关于记忆和遗忘的规则，反正以前是个谜。依我的大胆猜测，谜底其实也不太复杂。主管记住什么、忘记什么的中枢，听从的是情感的指令。我们天生愿意保存那些美好、善良、友谊、勇敢的事件，不爱记着那些丑恶、虚伪、背叛、怯懦的片段。当然，这并不是说人应该篡改真相，文过饰非虚情假意瞎编一气，只是想说明我们的心，好像一只美丽的小箱子，容量有限。当它储存物品的时候，经过了严格的挑选，把那些引起我们忧愁和苦闷的往事，留在了外面，保留的是亲情和友情。

我衷心希望每个人的小箱子里，都装满光明和友爱。

Our Heart is a Little Treasure Box

Learning to read at school, I marvelled at the great number of Chinese characters that contain the component "heart" (心). There are "miss"(念), "think" (想), "mean" (意), "forget" (忘), "be kind" (慈), "feel" (感), "lament" (愁), "ponder" (思), "be evil" (恶), "console" (慰) and "be wise" (慧), to name but a few. Alas, what a large family of characters with the "heart!"

Each of them has a "heart" lying quietly at the bottom as if forming their soulful foundation. Then there are the characters with an upright component, a "heart" closely to the left, such as "remember" (忆), "embrace" (怀), "hasten" (快), "fear"(怕), "blame" (怪), "annoy" (恼), "hate" (恨), "regret" (惭), "quieten"

(悄), "habituate" (惯), "cherish" (慌) and so on. I must stop or else risk being showy and pedantic.

Suffice to say, our ancestors, as we can imagine, had thought highly of "heart" when they invented the writing script. It was so important to them that merely putting it at the bottom was not nearly enough. It must have a rightful place to the left as well.

However, in human anatomy, the heart, an important organ, no less, is but a pump for getting blood to the rest of our body, itself having little to do with thinking. Having it associated with the words for mental activities and emotions is a misnomer.

In truth, it is the brain that governs our thinking.

The human brain is a marvel. Scholars have used phrases such as "the vast ocean of consciousness" to describe it. Yet our skull, if it could be compared to a pottery jar, has a volume not much larger than a large bottle of cola. With small children, it is even smaller; perhaps just several cans of soda. Yet, people use words like ocean to describe all that is under the hood — an ocean of huge swells and boundless expanses welcoming all rivers and streams that flow into it. Why is it so?

The brain is home to our emotions and wisdom. It governs our thinking and decision-making. It is capable of remembering and forgetting, which is not entirely subject to your will. You may have found a text that you were required to learn by heart so difficult to memorize however you tried. Even if you did manage to commit it to memory, you could still falter when asked by your teacher to recite it the following day, because you were all nerves in front of the class. You'd be flummoxed and scratch your head, but to no avail. If you were asked again a few months later, you'd be even hazier and hopelessly lost. Yet, something casually heard or seen, which didn't leave a dent at the moment, could be etched as if by magic in our memory forever.

I know not what scientists of late have learned about human memory. It used to be shrouded in mystery. But I can boldly guess the mystery is not that difficult to unravel. It is the emotions that affect our ability to remember information and recall past events. We are prone to cherish experiences of beauty, kindness, friendship and bravery, and block fragments of ugliness, deceit, betrayal and cowardice. It does not mean that people could alter, gloss over or reinvent past events, but rather our heart, like a little treasure box with finite capacity, is highly selective in what to keep, cherishing warmth and kindness of family and friendship, while keeping out sorrows and grief.

I heartily wish that the little treasure box in each of us could be brimful of affection and light.

帮助的人越多，幸福感越强

被人需要是很快乐的事情，很穷很忙而无力帮助别人的时候，内心的感觉便十分黯淡。

美国哥伦比亚大学的研究人员在调研中证明，给他人帮助越多的人，幸福感越强。帮助他人这一行为，本身自有其深远的影响。人们需要释放内心的人道主义情怀，在帮助或是施舍他人的时候，大脑的活动更为积极。

研究人员把一些钱装在信封里，分给一些学生，准确地说，是分给了四十六名加拿大学生，然后对他们说，你可以用这些钱给自己买些东西，或者是给别人买东西，送给他们。到了下午五点，研究人员把这批学生集合起来，调查其快乐指数。发现钱的多少，与快乐指数无关。不过那些给别人买东西的人，比给自己买东西的人，要快乐得多。

乍一听，怀疑真的是这样吗？多数人，还是给自己花了钱，比较舒服吧？然后假设自己做了这个实验。我想，我会选择把钱给我的父母，我的儿子，我的丈夫……这样想过之后，不禁哑然失笑。自己也是凡人，并不比别人更高尚或者更龌龊。所以，这实验的结果是真实的，结论通用你我。

研究证明，当人接受馈赠的时候，和给人帮助或施舍的时候，满足感是由大脑的同一部分产生的，只不过在帮助别人的时候，这一区域更为活跃。有时想，如果人的大脑皮层是透明的，我们就会看到，当那些神经活动的时候，我们会更有成就感。这是一个有趣的实验。

我相信，当一个人被他人需要的时候，是非常美妙的感受，成就感是无与伦比的。不信，你试一试。我会很乐意向人求助，因为这在给予自己机会的同时，也是给予了别人一个释放爱心的机会。我想，这恐怕是遗传给我们的精神馈赠。因为从远古时代起，只有那些愿意帮助别人的人，才会有更多的机会留下子嗣。我们基本是这种人的后代，在血液中就留下了良好的习惯。这种从心中捧出的、抛洒四处的爱意，我们要为之感动。

The More You Help Others, the Happier You Are

It is a joy to feel you are needed by others, even if you are very busy and poor. You feel glum when you find yourself unable to lighten the sorrow of others.

A study by researchers at Columbia University in the United States found that the more people helped others, the stronger their sense of well-being are. Here lies something of great, far-reaching significance to human life. We all have a deep innate need to care and be compassionate. While we are engaged in the act of giving and helping others, our brains become more activated.

The researchers randomly distributed envelopes containing

cash to some students, or to be more precise, to 46 Canadian students, who were told that they could spend the money buying either something for themselves or some gifts for others. At 5 p.m., they were reassembled by the researchers to rate their sense of happiness. It was found that the actual amount of money in envelopes had no impact on happiness, yet those who bought something for others enjoyed far greater happiness than those who did it for themselves.

On first hearing this, I doubted if it was true. Wouldn't most people feel better when buying stuff for themselves? Then I imagined myself being a participant in this experiment. I would probably have chosen to spend the money on something for my parents, son, husband ... I chuckled at such a reflection. I am a mere mortal, no meaner or nobler than another. Thus, the study seems convincing enough and should hold true for you and me.

Research has shown that when we are giving or receiving help or gifts, the feeling of gratification is activated in the same part of our brain. The only difference is that the stimulation is greater when we are cheerfully giving. It amuses me to imagine that should human cerebral cortex be transparent, we probably would have a greater sense of achievement when seeing the activated parts of our brain blinking sweetly. This indeed is an interesting study.

No doubt, helping someone in need always gives us the joyous glow. The sense of accomplishment is simply incomparable. You should give it a try if you are not so convinced. I am always happy to accept the gift of help, for while it opens up a window of opportunity for me, it also gives others a chance to show their generous heart. I further believe our giving and accepting is perhaps a gift of Mother Nature and the outcome of evolution. From ancient times, those who were generous in helping others would likely have better chances of survival and procreation. We are by and large all descendants of such ancient ancestors with the good-heartedness flowing in the blood. We marvel at such magnanimous, altruist traits and cannot help feeling deeply touched even to this day.

常常爱惜

拾起一穗遗落在秋天原野上的麦芒时，我们心中会涌起一种情感……

当水龙头正酝酿着滴落一颗椭圆形的水珠，一只手紧紧拧住闸门时，我们心中会涌起一种情感……

当凝望宝蓝的天空因为浓雾而浑浑噩噩时，我们心中会涌起一种情感……

当注视到一个正义的人无力捍卫自己的尊严，孤苦无助的时候，我们心中会涌起一种情感……

人类将这种痛而波动的感觉命名为——爱惜。

我们读这两个字的时候，通常要放低了声音，徐徐地从肺腑最柔软的孔腔吐出，怕惊碎了这薄而透明的温情。

爱惜的人前提是——爱。爱是人类一种最珍贵的体验，它发源于深刻的本能和绵绵的眷恋。爱先于任何其他情感，轻轻沁入婴儿小而玲珑的心灵。爱那给予生命的母亲，爱那清冷的空气和滑润的乳汁。爱温暖的太阳和柔和的抚爱，爱飞舞的光影和若隐若现的乐声……

爱惜的土壤是喜欢。当我们喜欢某种东西的时候，就期冀它的长久和广大，忧郁它的衰减和短暂。当我们对喜爱之物，怀有难以把握的忧虑之时，吝啬是一个常会首选的对策。我们会俭省珍贵的资源，我们会珍爱不可重复的时光，我们会制造机会以期重享愉悦，我们会细水长流反复咀嚼快乐。

于是，爱惜就在不知不觉中发生了。

当我们爱惜的时候，保护的勇气和奋斗的果敢也同时滋生。真爱，需用生命护卫。真爱，就会义无反顾。没有保护的爱惜，是朵无蕊鲜花，可以艳丽，却断无果实。没有爱惜的保护，是粗糙和逼人的威迫，是强权而不是心心相印。

爱惜常常发生。在我们不经意的时候，打湿眼帘。

爱惜好比一只竹篮。随着人类的进步，它越编越大了，盛着人自身，盛着绿色，盛着地球上所有的物种，盛着天空和海洋。

Pathos

It is what wells up when we pick up a lone ear of wheat in the autumn field ...

It is that feeling of ours when seeing a perfect droplet forming at the end of the spout as we turn off the tap ...

It is what we feel when gazing at the otherwise azure sky made opaque by smog ...

It is that reaction inside us when seeing an upright man alone and unable to defend his dignity ...

Pathos is that aching feeling we hold for what we dearly cherish. The word itself is often uttered in a lowered voice, akin to a sigh, quietly exhaled from this tender region in our chest,

17

for fear its airy sense of pity might just vanish into thin air.

Love underpins pathos. Love is the most precious of human experiences, tender and enduring, arising from a primal instinct. Love grows before all else in the little yet perfect heart of a newborn; love for its life-giving mother, the refreshing waft of cold air and the sweet, smoothing milk. There is also the love for the warm sun, the gentle touch on the skin, the dappled light dancing on the wall and the drifting strains of a song ...

Affection is the soil for pathos. When we hold something dear, we yearn for its growth and perpetuity, and lament its evanescence and demise. When we are anxious about possibly losing what we cherish, we become tight-fisted by default. We are sparing with precious resources and cherish the moments that can never be repeated. We find excuses to recreate delightful experiences of yore and savour the present moments of joy, hoping they could linger.

This is when pathos catches us unawares.

When we dearly cherish something, we become bold and

decisive in its defence. We guard love with life and total resolve. To love is to cherish, or else love would be flowers without pistils — glorious, but incapable of bearing fruits. Without the cherishing, love is vulnerable, riddled with crudeness and coercion; it is conquest by force, rather than that of heart.

The feeling of cherishing arises often without us even realizing it, bringing a glint of tears in our eyes.

Pathos is like an evolving web, growing bigger and bigger with the progress of humanity, encompassing all that is green, all the living creatures on earth, the fathomless skies and immense oceans, and all of us.

豆角鼓

有一个在幼儿园就熟识的朋友，男生。那时，我们同在一张小饭桌上吃饭。劳动课的时候，阿姨发给每人一面跳新疆舞用的小铃鼓，里头装满了豆角。当我择不完豆角丝的时候，他会来帮我。我们就把新疆铃鼓称为"豆角鼓"。

以后几十年，我们只有很少的来往，彼此都知道对方在城市的某一个角落里，愉快地生活着。一天，他妻子来电话，说他得了喉病，手术后在家静养，如果我有时间的话，请给他去个电话。我连连答应，说明天就做。他妻子略略停了一下说，通话时，请您尽量多说，他会非常入神地听。但是，他不会回答您，因为他无法说话。

第二天，我给他打了电话。当我说出他的名字以后，对方是长久的沉默。我习惯地等待着回答，猛然意识到，我是不可能得到回音的。我便自顾自地说下去，确知他就在电线的那一端，静静地聆听着。自言自语久了，没有反响也没有回馈，甚至连喘息的声音也没有，感觉很是怪异，好像你面对着无边无际的棉花垛……

那天晚上，他的妻子来电话说，他很高兴，很感谢，希望我以后常常给他打电话。

我答应了，但拖延了很长的时间。也许是因为那天独自说话没有回音的感受太特别了。后来，我终于再次拨通了他家的电话。当我说完，你是××吗？我是你幼儿园的同桌啊……

我停顿了一下，并不是等待他的回答，只是喘了一口气，预备兀自说下去。就在这个短暂的间歇里，我听到了细碎的哗啦啦声……这是什么响动？啊，是豆角鼓被人用力摇动的声音！

那一瞬，我热泪盈眶。人间的温情跨越无数岁月和命运的阴霾，将记忆烘烤得蓬松而馨香。

那一天，每当我说完一段话的时候，就有"哗啦啦"的声音响起，一如当年我们共同把择好的豆角倒进菜筐。当我说"再见"的时候，回答我的是响亮而长久的豆角鼓声。

Beanie Tambourine

This is a friend I have known since kindergarten. We always sat at the same little table at mealtimes. The kindergarten in our time taught kids various little skills and one was helping with kitchen chores. We'd be each given some green beans, dished out in a tambourine for Xinjiang dances. When I couldn't finish trimming all my beans, he would trot over to help out with what was left in the "beanie tambourine," a name we came up with together.

In the decades afterwards, we rarely saw each other, knowing only each of us living a life of contentment somewhere in the city. Then one day I got a call from his wife saying that he had just had a throat surgery and was recuperating at home. It would be so nice if I could give him a call when I had time. I agreed immediately and promised to make a call the next day. His wife then said after a pause, "When you call, please keep talking. He will be all ears. But he won't answer you as he has lost his voice."

I called the next day. After I called his name, there was a long silence on the other end of the line. I waited out of habit before it struck me that I would never hear anything back. I talked on as if to myself, knowing he was at the other end quietly listening. I soldiered on. No echoing, no feedback, not even the sound of a sigh. It felt weird as if you were talking to a mountain of cotton balls.

That evening, his wife called to tell me how happy and thankful he was and hoped that I would call from time to time.

I agreed but hesitated for a long time before the next call, probably because talking without hearing any response in the first call felt so odd. Then, at long last, I dialed his home number again. I paused after saying, "This is so and so. I am your desk mate at kindergarten … .," not to expect any reply but to take a deep breath before resuming my soliloquy. In the momentary silence, I heard some swishing, rustling sounds. What could that be? Then I realized it was the rattling of the beanie tambourine!

At that instant, my eyes brimmed with tears. Memories of childhood friendship flowed across long decades and life's many trials, warming us as it were with the glow of a crackling fire on a snowy night.

On that day, every pause in my soliloquy was filled by the rattling of the tambourine, just as it did when we emptied our trimmed beans into the large basket. When I ended with "Talk to you again," it was echoed by a resonant drumbeat on the beanie tambourine.

保持惊奇

惊奇，是天性的一种流露。

生命开始的一瞬就是惊奇。我们周围的世界，为什么由黑暗变得明朗？周围为什么由水变成了气？为什么由温暖变得清凉？外界的声音为何如此响亮？那个不断俯视我们、亲吻我们的女人是谁？

从此我们在惊奇中成长。

这个世界上，有多少值得惊奇的事情啊。苹果为什么落地？流星为什么"下雨"？人为什么兵戎相见？史为什么世代更迭？……

孩子大睁着纯洁的双眼，面对着未知的世界，不断地惊奇着、探索着，在惊奇中渐渐长大。

惊奇是幼稚的特权，惊奇是一张白纸。

但人是不可以总是惊奇着的。在生命的某一个时辰，你突然因为你的惊奇，遭逢尴尬与嘲笑。你惊奇地发现——惊奇在更多的时候，是稚弱的表现，是少见多怪的代名词，是一种原始蛮荒的状态。

对于我们这个崇尚"见怪不怪，其怪自败"，尊重老练成熟的民族心理中，惊奇是如胎发一般的标志。

你想成功吗？你首先须成功地把自己的惊奇掩盖起来。

我们的词典里，印着许多诸如"处变不惊""宠辱不惊"的词汇，使"不惊"镀着大将风度的光辉，而"惊"屈于永久的贬义。

翻那词典，后面更有了"惊慌失措""大惊失色""惊恐万状"的形容，惊堕落着，简直就是怯懦、退缩、畏葸的同义词了。

于是人们开始厌恶惊奇。你想做大事吗？一个必备的基本功就是训练自己丧失惊奇。

你看到爱情远不是传说中那般纯洁，你不要惊奇。

你看到生活远没有书本上描写的那么美好，你不要惊奇。

你看到友谊根本不是故事中那般忠诚，你不要惊奇。

你看到日子绝不如想象中那般绚烂，你不要惊奇……

如果你惊奇了，你就违反了一条透明的规则，会遭到别人阳光下或是暗影里的嘲笑：这个孩子还嫩着呢。

你在一次次碰壁后省悟到，即使你对这个世界还一知半解，你还搞不清问题的全部，但有一点你现在就能做到：埋葬你的惊奇。

你看到丑恶，假装没有看到，依旧面不改色、谈笑风生，人们就会送你"人情练达"的评价。你听到秽闻，仿佛在那一刻患了突发性的耳聋，脸上毫无表情，人们会感觉你老于世故、可以信赖。你被美丽、美好、美妙的景色感动，只可以默默地藏在心底，脸上切不可露出少见多怪的惊异，人们就会以为你少年老成，有大谋略、大气魄，是可做将帅的优良材料。你碰到可歌可泣的人间至情，要把心肠练得硬如钻石，脸不变色心不跳。就算真搅得肝肠寸断，只可夜晚躲在无人处暗自咀嚼，切不可叫人觑了去，落得个妇人之仁的罪名……

现代社会是一只飞速旋转的风火轮，把无数

信息强行灌输给我们。见怪不怪，我们的心灵渐渐在震颤中麻痹，更不消说有意识地掩饰我们的惊讶，会更猛烈地加速心灵粗糙。在灯红酒绿和人为的打磨中，我们必将极快地丧失掉惊奇的本能。

于是我们看到太多矜持的面孔，我们遭遇无数微笑后面的冷淡。我们把惊奇视作一种性格缺憾，我们以为永不惊讶才是人生的至高境界。

细细分析起来，惊奇是由两部分组成的，先有了惊，然后才是奇。如果说"惊"属于一种对陌生事物认识局限的愕然，"奇"则是对未知事物积极探讨的萌芽了。

否认了"惊"，就扼杀了它的同胞兄弟。我们将在无意之中，失去众多丰富自己的机遇。

假如牛顿不惊奇，他也许就把那个包裹着真理的金苹果吃到自己的小肚子里面了，人类与伟大的"万有引力定律"相逢，也许还要迟滞很多年。

假如瓦特不惊奇，水壶盖"噗噗"响着，一个划时代的发现就蒸发到厨房的空气中了，我们的蒸汽火车头，也许还要在牛车漫长的辙道里蹒跚亿万公里。

即使对普通人来说，掩盖惊奇，也易闹笑话。一位乡下朋友，第一次住进城里的宾馆。面对盥洗室里那些式样别致的洁具，他想不通人洗一个脸，何至于要如此麻烦。他不会使用这些物件，本来请教一下服务小姐，也就迎刃而解了。可是他不想暴露自己的惊奇，就用地上一个雪白的盛着半盆水的瓷器洗了脸，后来他才知道，那是马桶。

这当然是一个极端的例子，我把它写在这里，绝无幸灾乐祸之意。现代社会令人眼花缭乱，每个人在某种意义上说都是孤陋寡闻的。你在你的行业里是行家里手，在其他领域完全可能是白痴。这不是羞愧的事情，坦率地流露惊奇，表示自己对这一方面的无知以及求知的探索，是一种可嘉的勇气。

我认识一位老人，一天兴致勃勃地同我探讨电脑的种种输入方法。他整整八十二岁了，肾脏功能已经衰竭，我坚信他这一辈子也不可能在电脑键盘上敲出一个字。他在自己的专业范畴里，是一位德高望重的长者，但对电脑的理解多有谬误，就连我这个"二把刀"也听出了许多破绽。但是老人家充满探索之光的惊奇的眼神，在这一瞬像探照灯一样扫过我的灵魂。面对他青筋暴突、微微颤抖的手，我想，不知我这一生可否活得这样高寿？不论我生命的历程有多长，我一定要记得这目光炯炯的惊奇，学习他对世界的这份挚爱，绝不仅仅流连在熟悉的航道，要始终保持对辽阔海域的探索，直到我最后一次呼吸。

惊奇是一种天然物，而不是制造出来的，它是真情实感的火花。一块滚圆的鹅卵石便不再会惊讶于江河的波涛，惊奇蕴涵着奋进的活力。

惊奇不仅仅是幼稚，惊奇不仅仅是无知，惊奇是在它们基础上的深化和前进。

你既然惊奇了，你就要探索这奥妙；你既然惊奇了，你就不能仅仅止于惊奇。爱好惊奇的人须将惊奇转化为平凡。消灭惊奇的过程，也就是学习的过程，惊奇在熟悉中淡化，才干在惊奇中成长。

世界是没有止境的，惊奇也是没有止境的。惊奇是流动的水，它使我们的思想翻滚着，散发着清新，抗拒着腐烂。

在城市里待得久了，常常使我们丧失惊奇的本能。我们像鳝一样滑行着，浑身粘满市侩的黏液。

到自然中去，造化永远给我们以大惊喜。和寥廓的宇宙相比，个人的得失是怎样的微不足道啊。不要小看山水的洗涤，假如真正同天地对一次话，我们定会惊奇自己重新获得活力。

如果无法到自然中去，就同与自己没有利害关系的从小的朋友，做一次促膝的谈心。利害关系这件事，实在是交友的大敌。我不相信有永久的利益，我更珍视患难与共的友谊。长留史册的，不是锱铢必较的利益，而是肝胆相照的情分。和朋友坦诚地交往，会使我们留存着对真情的敏感，会使我们的眼睛抹去云翳，心境重新开朗，惊奇就在这清明的心境中，翩翩来临了。

假如既没有自然可以依傍，又没有朋友可以信赖，那真是人生的大憾事。那只有在静夜中同自己对话，回忆那些经历中最美好的片段，温习曾经使心灵震撼的镜头。它也许是很小的一朵旷野里的花，也许是冬天的一盏红灯笼，也许是苍茫的大漠暮色，也许是雄浑激荡的乐曲……总之，那是独属于你的一份秘密，只有你才知道它对于你的惊奇的意义。《论语》里说："学而时习之，不亦说乎？"复习以往我们情感中最精彩的片段，常常会使我们整旧如新。

保持惊奇，我常常这样对自己说。它是一眼永不干涸的温泉，会有汨汨的对世界的热爱蒸腾而起，滋润着我们的心灵。

33

Never Lose Your Sense of Wonder

Our sense of wonder is a gift of nature.

It is triggered at the moment of our birth — the sense of awe at the world that is suddenly filled with light. Why does the water that has surrounded us change into the air? Why is the warmth being replaced by coolness? What are all the loud sounds? Who is this woman gazing at me and not stop kissing me?

We grow ever after with this sense of wonder.

Indeed, how the world is filled with wonders! Why do apples fall down to the ground? Why do shooting stars fall down from the sky? Why do humans go to war and kingdoms rise and fall?

The starry-eyed child grows up with his sense of wonder, exploring the unknown and never ceasing to be amazed.

To wonder is a privilege of the naïve. It is a blank page waiting to be filled.

Yet, you are not supposed to wonder and be awed all the time. At a certain point in life, you may suddenly find yourself being embarrassed or ridiculed for your childlike wonder. You come to the shocking realization that having a sense of wonder can be deemed weakness; a euphemism for being ignorant, a philistine, and the savagely unenlightened.

In a culture like ours that values the equable, inured and those who are surprised at nothing, having a sense of wonder is akin to being not dry behind the ears.

To get ahead in life, you will have to first learn

to conceal your sense of wonder.

In our age-old dictionary, "being in wonder or awe" is a pejorative, in contrast to being "unruffled in moments of crisis" and "unperturbed by glory or humiliation;" all edifying attributes befitting an audacious general.

If we look further, we may find in that dictionary phrases for "be panic-stricken," "turn pale with fear," and "be frightened out of one's wits" all contained the same Chinese character for "awe," connoting the sense of cowardice, retreat and fear.

Thus, people have come to detest "awe." If you want to get somewhere, you have to train yourself not to be awed, daunted, or surprised.

Thus, you shouldn't be surprised if love is not as pure as the legend has it.

You shouldn't fume if life is not as sublime as books have made you believe.

You shouldn't agonize when friends are not as loyal as they do in stories.

You are supposed to be cool as you trudge through the

daily grind that is anything but glorious ...

If you look surprised and dare to question, you have broken the unspoken rule. You would be scoffed at either to your face or behind your back — you are barely out of short pants. You have learned after many a snub and setback that even though you only have a half-baked understanding of things and are yet to learn to see the big picture, there is one thing you should do without delay: conceal your sense of wonder and let nothing astonish you.

You pretend seeing no evil and carry on the show, doling out your charm, unruffled. Then you earn the repute of a sophisticate, a man of the world. When there is any ugly news, you act as if you suffer a temporary hearing loss. Your unfazed look will then be taken as stoic resignation, a mark of the trustworthy. Even when you are touched by the beauty, grace and magnificence in the landscape, you keep it bottled up, never letting your sense of awe be shown. Then, you will be thought of as deliberate, ambitious, and wise beyond your years, cut out to be a leader. When you are touched by great affection and compassion, you act as if you have a heart of stone. You certainly don't wear it on your sleeve and will do your agonizing out of the sight, if you are so shaken to the core or feel like eating your heart out, or else risk being seen as sissy and wimpy.

In the rapidly turning whirlpool that is our contemporary society, we are overwhelmed by ubiquitous information. Our mind grows dull under its overload. We also rapidly become numb and insensitive deep within as we try hard to conceal our sense of wonder. Through the mindless pursuit of sensory delights and self-inflicted deprivation, we sooner or later will lose our capacity for wonder altogether.

Thus we see so much pose and dissimulation around us, the indifference and cold shoulder despite the courtesy of half smiles. Having a sense of wonder is reduced to character weakness, while being surprised at nothing is deemed the ultimate expression of panache.

If you look at the Chinese phrase for "a sense of wonder," it is comprised of two characters: "surprise" and "amazement." The former connotes a sense of awe at the unusual and strange thanks to limitations of prior experience, while the latter borders on an urge to actively explore the unknown.

Take out that element of surprise and awe and you stifle its twin brother — the urge to explore. In so doing, you miss opportunities for enriching experiences; to live life to the full.

Should Isaac Newton not have had his sense of wonder, he might have simply eaten that fallen apple, golden with truth, and that would be that. Humanity's discovery of the law of universal gravitation would have to wait for many years.

If James Watt had not been amazed by the steam pushing up the lid of the kettle, the invention of the steam engine, an epoch-making event, would have gone into the air of his kitchen, with the inconsequential steam. The wheels of humanity's progress would have been bogged down in millions of more miles of ox-wagon ruts.

For ordinary folks, concealing your surprise sometimes could simply make you look like a fool. As one story goes, a country bumpkin once checked into a hotel for the first time in his life. He was dumbfounded when seeing all the fancy bathroom fixtures. He couldn't understand why there should be so much trouble for a simple wash of his face. He could have asked the housekeeping attendant. Yet he did not want to reveal his puzzlement. He went for the half-filled porcelain bowl in the corner for a wash of his face, not realizing till later its intended use.

This, of course, is an extreme case. I have no intention of taking delight in the hapless fellow's mishap by bringing it up here. To a certain extent, we are all limited in our knowledge, given all the confounding changes in modern society. You can claim expertise in one field, but be dumb as a post in another.

This is not something to be ashamed of. Show your amazement and frankly admit your ignorance and your desire to learn. This in itself is already commendable courage.

An elder whom I know well once had an enthused discussion with me on various input methods for the computer. This was an 82-year-old man who suffered renal failure. I thought that he probably would never have a chance to type a single character on the computer for the rest of his life. A highly respected scholar in his field, his knowledge of the computer was patchy. Even a novice like me could tell the many flaws in his understanding. Yet I was struck by the sparkle of wonder and curiosity in his eyes. I was shaken to the core. Looking at his shaky, sinewy hands, I wondered if I would ever live to his ripe old age. Yet, no matter how long the rest of my life's journey will be, I will never forget his shining eyes and his sense of wonder. I will try to emulate his passion for life and keep exploring the vast unknown, never settling for less — retreating into the comfort of the familiar — until my last breath.

Our sense of wonder is inborn, a gift of nature rather than an acquired trait. It is the fiery spark of genuine feeling. It moves us so and we strive and explore, not letting our instincts be dimmed, like round pebbles settling in still water with their joys in surging waves but a faint memory.

The sense of wonder is much more than childlike naivety or ignorance. It grows from them and then transcends them.

You yearn to explore when you are awed. As your curiosity is piqued, you will not stop at merely wondering. You must find out more and turn the unknown into known. In so doing, you acquire skills, prowess and knowledge, as the strange and unusual becomes the familiar.

The world is full of wonder and endlessly evolving. We should never lose our sense of wonder. Ceaseless like flowing water, it keeps our mind forever active, refreshed and immune to decay.

Living in a city for too long may dim our sense of wonder. We grow disenchanted, bored and cynical, slippery as an eel.

Get out into nature — the world of all that is beautiful and awe-inspiring. Our little calculations and preoccupation become so paltry and insignificant in the immenseness of nature. Belittle not the cathartic effects of being in contact with nature. You will be surprised by how energized you become if you can truly be in dialogue with nature.

If you cannot get out into nature for now, try to have a good heart-to-heart with a pal from childhood who shares your friendship not out of expediency. A friendship driven by expediency is doomed because it never lasts. I cherish friendships that have been through trials and hardships. Genuine camaraderie, free from calculation and quid pro quo, is remembered forever. We remain sensitive to true emotions and affection in an honest and sincere friendship. Our eyes are unclouded and our heart open. In such a refreshed and clear state of mind, we regain our sense of wonder.

Should we be so sadly deprived, neither being able to go into nature nor having a friend to turn to, we can still have an inner dialogue, reminiscing on a quiet night the most beautiful of our experiences — the moments that touched our soul. It could be seeing a tiny flower alone in a vacant expanse of field, a blazingly red lantern in a cold winter night, sunset in a vast, empty desert, or some powerful, uplifting strains of a song. Whatever it may be, it must be something most endearing to you alone; with the power to inspire your sense of wonder and awe. To quote from *The Analects*, "Isn't it a delight to study and review what you have learned?" Revisiting the most uplifting moments in our past emotional experiences nourishes us and makes us start anew.

I often say to myself, "Never lose your sense of wonder." It is an everlasting wellspring of strength and warmth, both nourishing and inspiring to our soul, welling up in us a powerful love for this world.

你要好好爱自己

你要好好爱自己。

这话来自一句叮嘱。最早向我们说起它的人，可能是我们的父母，可能是我们的师友，可能是我们的恋人爱人……

他们也许会一而再再而三地说：冷了要添衣，热了要洗脸。不要熬夜，不要一忙就忘了吃饭。要和大家伙儿搞好关系，要对得起自己的良心……要早睡早起……

如果从来没有人对你说起过这些絮絮叨叨啰啰唆唆的话，那你的童年和少年加上青年时期，孤寂荒凉。你未曾被人捧在手心，极少承接过温情。

不过，这没什么了不起的。因为无论别人怎样对你说这些话，说过多少次，都是身外之物。话音终将袅袅远去，要紧的是——你要自己对自己说这句话——你要好好爱自己。在纷杂人间的清朗月夜，你要耳语般但无比坚定地对自己说。

好好爱自己，是简单朴素的常识。可是这世上有多少人，能够懂得能够记住能够做到呢？

放眼四周，谬爱种种。

有人年轻时不顾死活拼命挣钱，预约给自己年老的时候可以肆意享乐，放开一搏。他们以为这就是爱自己了。

有人以为给自己的胃填进一些过多的食物，让罕见的山珍野味把肚腹撑得两眼翻白，这就是爱自己了。

有人以为在手腕上箍住名表，在颈项间悬挂重磅的金饰，这就是爱自己了。

有人以为把身体安置在一个庞大的屋舍内，再用很多名牌将自己掩埋，这就是爱自己了。

有人以为把自己的腿最大限度地闲置起来，抵达任何一个地方都由汽油和钢铁代步，这就是爱自己了。

有人以为让自己的外貌和自己的内脏年龄不相符，让面容在层层化妆品的粉饰下，显出不合时宜的嫩相。严重者不惜刀兵相见大胆斧正自我，甚至可以将腿骨敲断以求延展下肢增加身高，就是狠狠地爱自己了。

有人以为让嘴巴说言不由衷之话，让表情肌做不是发自内心的谄媚之态，让双膝弯曲，让目光羞于见人，这都是爱自己。

实际情况恰恰相反，以上诸等，皆是对不起自己，害了自己。

爱自己是需要理由的。我们的爱要想持之以恒，先要明白自己究竟是谁。

最明确的结论是——自己首先是一个身体。这个身体结构精巧，机能完善，高度发达，精美绝伦。千百万年进化的水流，将身体打磨成健全而温润的宝石。

大脑的功用是思考，而不是他人任意抛洒塑料袋的垃圾场。凡事用自己的脑袋想一想，做出最合乎理性的决定，这就是对自己的脑袋好。

眼睛要看洁净美好之物，看出潜在的危险找到安全方向。眼睛还有小小的癖好，爱看草木的绿色和天空的湛蓝，爱看书本和笑靥。满足它的愿望，非礼勿视，这就是对眼睛好。

鼻子希望呼吸到清新的空气，闻到花香，不喜欢密不通风的腐朽之气和穹顶之下皆是雾霾。让它远离这样的环境，才是对鼻子的爱惜。

嘴巴希望讲的都是发自内心的真话，摄入富有营养的本色食品，而不是混杂三聚氰胺和地沟油的伪劣食物。不说口是心非的谗言，嘴唇上翘，嘴巴就微笑了。

双手希望能通过自己的劳动创造出美好生活的物质基础，而不是扒窃抢劫和杀戮。这就是手的幸运了。

我们的脏腑希望它能劳逸结合，不要总是爆满，不要连轴转。要有张有弛劳逸结合。不要被塞进太多赘物，不要无端地损耗它们的能量。

颈椎希望能不时地扬起头，舒展它弯曲的弧度。而不是终日保持一个僵硬的姿势，以至于每一节间隙都缩窄，过度摩擦增生长出骨刺。

脊骨希望自己能够庄严地挺直，快乐向前。这不但是生理的需要，也是心理的需要。一个卑躬屈膝的人，谈不上尊严。而没有尊严的人，不会好好对待自己。因为他看不起自己，以为自己只是蝼蚁。

我们的肩膀，希望能担负一定的担子。不要太轻，那样就失去了肩负的责任；也不能太重，超过了负荷，肩周就会发炎。

双脚，希望坚稳地站立在大地之上。那种为了显示自己比实际高度更高的内外增高鞋，骨子里是虐待双脚的刑具。

我们的双腿，希望能在正当的道路上挺进。时而可以疾跑，时而可以漫步，时而可以暂停，倾听婉转莺啼。

我们的皮肤，希望能顺畅地呼吸，而不是被厚厚的脂粉糊满，戴一张石灰盔甲。

我们的头发，希望按照它的本来面目，风中舒展。黑就是黑，白就是白，黄就是黄。而不是像鸡毛掸子似的五颜六色，被反复弯曲和拉直，好像它是多变的小人。

我们的心脏，希望匀速地跳动。运动的时候可以适时加快，睡眠的时候，可以轻柔缓舒。需要拍案而起的时候，它可以剧烈搏动，以输出更多的血液，支撑我们怒发冲冠的豪气。千钧一发的时刻，它可以气壮山河地泵出极多血液，以提供给我们叱咤风云顶天立地的力量。

我惊叹人体的奥秘，大自然是何等慷慨地把最伟大的恩赐降临于我们身体之内。身体的每一个细枝末节，都遵循颇有深意的蓝图构建起来并完整地传承，兢兢业业一丝不苟。

只有爱自己的人，才有可能爱别人，一屋不扫，何以扫天下？一个不爱自己的人，断不会心细如发地爱别人。爱己爱人都是一种能量，它不是与生俱来，而是通过感知和模仿，通过领悟和学习，才慢慢积聚起来，直至蔚然成风。这世上有太多的人，不爱自己，第一个证据就是他们成了身体的叛徒。他们视身体是一团与己无关的肮脏抹布。

所有人的身体，都理应洁净而温暖。不仅儿童和青年圣美，中老年人的身体也依旧是和煦与高贵的。纵使曾经被侮辱与损害，有负罪之人为之承责，身体是无辜的。那些以为只有童子才清爽、处女才芬芳的念头，来自人性的无知和男权的霸道。

不过，这并不是好好爱自己的全部。在身体里，还有无比尊贵的主宰，那就是我们的灵魂。

爱惜灵魂，是好好爱自己的最高阶段。

人说灵魂有二十一克重，说在死亡的那一瞬间，灵魂会飞向天空。我不知道这个说法是否科学，但我相信在美好的身体里，一定安住着同样精彩的灵魂。它是人类最优秀的价值观之总和，是我们瞭望世界的支点。它凝聚了人类所信仰、所尊崇、所畏惧和所仰视的一切，在肉体之上，放射明亮光芒，穿透风雨迷蒙照耀着引导着我们。

　　如果这一世，你能爱惜身体珍重灵魂，那么从这个港口出发你会成为一叶身心平和的幸福小舟，一步步安然向前，驶入珍爱他人、珍爱万物、珍爱世界的宽广大海。

Genuinely Love Yourself

You must love yourself enough and deeply.

This may have been first said to us with caring concern by our parents, or a mentor, a dear friend, our better half ...

Untiringly, they tell you to bundle up when it gets nippy or splash your face with water when it is hot. They urge us not to burn midnight oil or miss our meals when we are overwhelmed with work. Learn to get along with everyone and be true to ourselves. Go to bed early and get up early ... So they would go on and on.

Yet if you have never been so endlessly nagged, you probably have had a rather lonely childhood and youth, without being dearly loved and deprived of the soothing comfort of cooing voice and gentle touch.

Such is life. Yet, even those words of caring concern, no matter how often they were said to you, are but external and will be behind you soon enough. What is important is that you say to yourself: Genuinely love yourself — under your breath perhaps but resolutely, alone on a quiet night when the whole world is in a rush.

The power of self-love is simple, common knowledge. Yet, how many understand it properly and take it to heart? How many ever succeed in doing it?

Look around us and we see all the wrong sorts of self-love.

Those who drive themselves into the ground to make money when they are young, hoping only to enjoy life fully when they get older, think that is self-love.

Those who gorge themselves on wild game and delicacies, pushing the gastric envelope until what went down were about to come back up, think that is self-love.

Those who have their wrist cuffed with fancy watches, or their neck weighed down with enormous gold jewellery, think that is self-love.

Those who dwell in enormous houses, and surround themselves with merchandise of big-name brands, think that is self-love.

Those who keep their feet idle and let a heap of steel and petrol move them, wherever they go, think that is self-love.

Then there are those who insist that their faces shouldn't look the age of their internal organs, putting on layers of makeup for the unseemly youthfulness. The staunchest of them even resort to the surgeon's lancet for cosmetic alteration. Or it could be a limb surgery with their leg bones being broken in two just to get that extra bit of body height. Indeed, they also think it is just a little self-love.

Then there are those who speak not from the heart,

striking a servile posture with the obsequious knees and the wandering eyes of a toady. For self-love, so they assume.

In fact, they do exactly the opposite. Rather than self-love, they render themselves a disservice and harm.

Self-love will not endure without self-knowledge. You have to know yourself before you can accept and love yourself.

Without a doubt, we are first and foremost physical beings. But what a marvellous being it is! A miracle of evolution, with an exquisite constitution and remarkable functions all in an incomparable package. The human body, the jewel, is the sublimation of millions of years of evolution.

Our brain, too, is marvellously built — for thinking. So use it to make the most rational decisions. You wouldn't let anyone walk through your mind dumping their plastic junk. This is to take good care of your brain.

Your eyes help you discern beauty and goodness, alert you to lurking danger and guide you onto a safe path. They take to the lush green, the infinite blue, the tantalizing lines of a book and the sunshine of smiles. Satisfy such desires and turn away from the base and improper. This is to take good care of your sight.

Your nose is made to take in the clean and fresh air and to sniff the scent of blossoms. It cringes in stale and musty air and the pervasive smog under heaven. Keep away from what it is adverse to and treat it well.

Speak from your heart. Eat real, nutritious food and guard yourself against the toxic food that is contaminated by the so-called gutter oil or melamine. Do not let slanderous words pass your lips, nor should you ever speak with a forked tongue. Lift the corners of your mouth and smile.

Our hands are made for productive work. That is the foundation of a happy life. If our hands can be put to such use, it is indeed a blessing. Never should they be used to take another's life or what is not ours.

Apply moderation with regard to food, drink, and work so as not to stress our internal organs, waste their energy or exhaust our body. Strike a balance between work and play and don't burn the candle at both ends. Don't gorge yourself.

Raise your head and stretch yourself from time to time so that you don't have that stiff, poor posture all day. Otherwise, you will suffer neck injury over time with spinal cord compression and bone spurs.

Your back should be straight so that you stand firm and upright, both in stature and in spirit. A cringing person has nothing in the way of self-respect. Those without self-respect never treat themselves well because of their self-loathing and deprecation.

We should shoulder appropriate responsibility; not so light as to be not meaningful, nor so heavy as to cause excessive stress, leading to inflammation.

We stand with our feet squarely on the ground. The elevated insoles or heels that make us look taller are nothing short of torture.

We stride with vigour on the right path, with a measured pace, quickening to a sprint or slowing down to a stroll as required, pausing and lingering from time to time to listen to the sounds of nature — the chorus of songbirds.

Our skin should breathe freely, not suffocated by powder and cream which cake like a chalky shield.

Our hair should have its natural colour and glow, rather than being dyed like fiery avian plumage, or curled and straightened over and again, forced into contorted forms like malleable clay dough.

Our heart keeps a steady pace, quickening as we exercise and slowing down as we repose. When we see injustice, our heart races to pump more blood and embolden us in our crimson-faced indignation. Our heart beats with powerful determination, as we stand tall in the moment of truth.

I marvel at the mystery of the human body, rich with nature's magnanimous endowment. It is a magical machine constructed meticulously down to the finest detail, following a design of profound meaning and replicated perfectly time and again.

Only when you love yourself can you love others. Charity begins with yourself. If you do not love yourself, you really cannot love others thoroughly and subtly. Self-love and love for another are both positive energy that can only be acquired through divination and learning over time until it is part of you. It is not something you are born with. The world is full of people without self-love. They are renegades of their own nature-endowed body. Their first symptom is a dislike for their own body, treating it with disdain as if it were a piece of rag.

Our body should be clean and well-clad. There is a sacred beauty in the child or youthful body;

there's also warmth and grace in the middle-aged and elderly. Even the bodies of those who have been harmed and victimized are innocent and beyond blame, while only the criminals and their culprits should be condemned. The notion that there is innocence and purity only in children and virgins is nothing but an expression of ignorance and boorish male chauvinism.

Yet, all this is partial self-love. There is something supreme — our soul — in every one of us.

Care for our soul is the pinnacle of self-love.

The soul is said to weigh exactly 21 grams which departs the body at the moment of one's demise. I am not sure if such a proposition is at all scientific. However, I'd like to believe that in the marvellous living human body there should be an equally marvellous soul — the sum of the finest human values and a viewpoint for looking at the world. It is the epitome of human beliefs, aversions, fears, and aspirations. It is the beacon light, more brilliant and higher than our mortal being, guiding us forward through the darkness of storm and rain.

Be comfortable in your own skin and take good care of

your soul, and you will be well provisioned to set sail. You will be blessed with peace in this life and achieve harmony of body and soul. Your vessel will stay a steady course, sailing into the generous ocean of greater love and compassion for all creatures great and small.

造心

蜜蜂会造蜂巢。蚂蚁会造蚁穴。人会造房屋、机器，造美丽的艺术品和动听的歌。但是，对于我们最重要最宝贵的东西——自己的心，谁是它的建造者？

孔雀绚丽的羽毛，是大自然物竞天择造出。白杨笔直刺向碧宇，是密集的群体和高远的阳光造出。清香的花草和缤纷的落英，是植物吸引昆虫繁衍后代的本能造出。卓尔不群、坚忍顽强的性格，是禀赋的优异和生活的历练造出。

我们的心，是长久地、不知不觉地以自己的双手，塑造而成。

造心先得有材料。有的心是用钢铁造的，沉黑无比。有的心是用冰雪造的，高洁酷寒。有的心是用丝绸造的，柔滑飘逸。有的心是用玻璃造的，晶莹脆薄。有的心是用竹子造的，锋利多刺。有的心是用木头造的，安稳麻木。有的心是用红土造的，粗糙朴素。有的心是用黄连造的，苦楚不堪。有的心是用垃圾造的，面目可憎。有的心是用谎言造的，百孔千疮。有的心是用尸骸造的，腐恶熏天。有的心是用眼镜蛇唾液造的，剧毒凶残。

造心要有手艺。一只灵巧的心，缝制得如同金丝荷包。一罐古朴的心，醇厚得好似百年老酒。一颗机敏的心，感应快捷电光石火。一颗潦草的心，门可罗雀疏可走马。一摊胡乱堆就的心，乏善可陈杂乱无章。一片编织荆棘的心，暗设机关处处陷阱。一道半是细腻半是马虎的心，好似白蚁蛀咬的断堤。一个绣花枕头内里虚空的心，是假冒伪劣心界的水货。

造心需要时间。少则一分一秒，多则一世一生。片刻而成的大智大勇之心，未必就不玲珑。久拖不决的谨小慎微之心，未必就很精致。有的人，小小年纪，就竣工一颗完整坚实之心。有的人，须发皆白，还在心的地基挖土打桩。有的人，半途而废不了了之，把半成品的心扔在荒野。有的人，成百里半九十，丢下不曾结尾的工程。有的人，精雕细刻一辈子，临终还在打磨心的剔透。有的人，粗制滥造一辈子，人未远行，心已灶冷坑灰。

心的边疆，可以造得很大很大。像延展性最好的金箔，铺设整个宇宙，把日月包含。没有一片乌云，可以覆盖心灵辽阔的疆域。没有哪次地震火山，可以彻底颠覆心灵的宏伟建筑。没有任何风暴，可以冻结心灵深处喷涌的温泉。没有某种天灾人祸，可以在秋天，让心的田野颗粒无收。

心的规模，也可能缩得很小很小，只能容纳一个家、一个人、一粒芝麻、一个病毒。一丝雨，就把它淹没了。一缕风，就把它粉碎了。一句流言，就让它痛不欲生。一个阴谋，就置它万劫不复。

心可以很硬，超过人世间已知的任何一款金属。心可以很软，如泣如诉如绢如帛。心可以很韧，千百次的折损委屈，依旧平整如初。心可以很脆，一个不小心，顿时香消玉碎。

造心的时候，可以有很多讲究和设计。

比如预埋下一处心灵的生长点，像一株植物，具有自动修复、自我养护的神奇功能。心受了创伤，它会挺身而出，引导心休养生息，在最短的时间内，使心整旧如新。

比如高高竖起心灵的避雷针，以便在危急时刻，将毁灭性的灾难导入地下，耐心等待雨过天晴。

比如添加防震防爆的性能，在心灵遭受短时间高强度的残酷打击下，举重若轻，镇定地维持蓬勃稳定。

比如……

优等的心，不必华丽，但必须坚固。因为人生有太多的压榨和当头一击，会与独行的心灵，在暗夜狭路相逢。如果没有精心的特别设计，简陋的心，很易横遭伤害一蹶不振，也许从此破罐破摔，再无生机。没有自我康复本领的心灵，是不设防的大门。一汪小伤，便漏尽全身膏血。一星火药，便可烧毁绵延的城堡。

心为血之海，那里汇聚着每个人的品格智慧精力情操，心的质量就是人的质量。有一颗仁慈之心，会爱世界爱人爱生活，爱自身也爱大家。有一颗自强之心，会勤学苦练百折不挠，宠辱不惊大智若愚。有一颗尊严之心，会珍惜自然善待万物。有一颗流量充沛羽翼丰满的心，会乘上幻想的航天飞机，抚摸月亮的肩膀。

造心是一项艰难漫长的工程，工期也许耗时一生。通常是母亲的手，在最初心灵的模型上，留下永不消退的指纹。所以普天下为人父母者，要珍视这一份特别庄重的义务与责任。

当以我手塑我心的时候，一定要找好样板，郑重设计，万不可草率行事。造心当然免不了失败，也很可能会推倒重来。不必气馁，但也不可过于大意。因为心灵的本质，是一种缓慢而精细的物体，太多的揉搓，会破坏它的灵性与感动。

　　造好的心，如同造好的船。当它下水远航时，蓝天在头上飘荡，海鸥在前面飞翔，那是一个神圣的时刻。会有台风，会有巨涛，但一颗美好的心，即使巨轮沉没，它的颗粒也会在海浪中，无畏而快乐地燃烧。

The Making of Our Heart

Bees make hives; ants nests. Humans build houses and machines, create exquisite works of art and weave many a pretty song. What then makes our heart which is the most important and precious to us all?

A peacock's dazzling plumage is the result of evolution. The tall aspens, with their straight, pillar-like trunks, reach skyward as they compete for sunlight in dense groves. The sweet scents and changing colours of flowers stem from plants' needs for reproduction. The uniqueness of our character and resilience grows from our natural endowments and through life's many trials.

As for our heart, the hand that shapes it is our very own, and the shaping happens unceasingly without us even knowing it.

What marks a good heart is its timbre. A heart of steel is rugged and toughened. A heart of ice is cold and haughty. A heart of velvet is soft and subtle. A heart of glass is easily shattered. Some have a heart of bamboo, sharp with splinters, while others of timber, steady yet dull. Some have a simple, coarse heart as if of red clay, while others are weighed down with sorrow, sour as a lemon. Then there are ugly hearts leaky with lies or laden with trash, prone to rot and decay, not to mention the vicious that are nothing but vile poison like cobra venom.

Then there is the question of subtlety and sophistication. A sensitive heart is like a silky satchel, finely embroidered in gold thread. A kindly, artless heart has the rich smoothness of an aged wine; while the heart of the witty is light, quick as a hare. A careless heart can't keep hold of what is dear and precious, while a messy heart is a jumbled collection of unsorted curios. A cunning heart deceives, leading others astray while the negligent and half-hearted are simply a disaster waiting to happen, like a dam infested with termites. The heart of the pretentious — being all fur coat and no knickers — is vain, a counterfeit paraded as the real thing.

Our heart may have to be shaped through a lifetime or indelibly marked in brief moments. A heart of valour and wisdom that is etched at the moment of truth is nonetheless of a fine order, while a heart of indecisiveness and timidity may not necessarily be delicate and subtle. Some may have a heart of resolve at a tender age, while others may still be blundering even though already being a grey old man. Some abandon their blotched attempt at character-building altogether while others give up their unfinished journey in the final stretch. Some dedicate their entire lives to attain the elusive transcendence of heart, not stopping till the very end, while the callous and brash may lose heart even as they have barely started.

The heart can be magnanimous and immense, boundless as the universe, with stars swirling in all expanding dimensions, shimmering as if on an edgeless gold leaf. No clouds darken it entirely; no temblor or volcano can topple its palatial superstructures. There may be storm and snow, but this wellspring of strength and warmth gurgles on. There is no calamity that such heart cannot weather, be it man-made or natural.

But the heart can also be small, accommodating no more than our family or a single person, or be filled to the brim by merely a petty thought, a vile virus. A drop of rain can drench it and a slight breeze can crumple it. A rumour may crush it; a single mischief may throw it into the eternal gloom.

The heart can be strong, tougher than the hardest steel. The heart can also be gentle, sensitive and soft as silk. A resilient heart endures, weathering storms and trials unscathed. A brittle heart can be fragile; crumpling to a thousand pieces by any slight or neglect.

There can be many designs and devices to make our heart strong.

Some capacity for self-healing and self-renewal, that magical power in a plant, for example, could come in handy for the heart. Such capacity will help our heart to recover and regain equilibrium within the shortest time possible after it has been hurt.

The heart also needs something like a lightning rod, for example, that conducts the lightning — catastrophic damages — to the ground at all the critical moments until the storm is over.

It can also be reinforced, as if a building being earthquake- or blast-proved, to withstand severe blows and persevere, calmly and unruffled.

The list could go on...

A good heart, shying away from the superfluous, must be resilient and strong. There bound to be oppression and blunt blows in life, as well as dire encounters with adversaries on a narrow path in the darkness of night. Without a well-instituted shield, a simple, unguarded heart could be easily hurt and broken, and become hopeless and reckless. A heart incapable of self-healing is an unguarded castle; easily reduced to ruins by a determined enemy. A small wound could cause the body to bleed to death; a small spark could set a fortress on fire if they were to be defenceless.

Our heart is the source of our character, wisdom, energy and moral strength. The quality of our heart is the measure of our worth as human beings. A kind, compassionate heart embraces the world, our loved ones and life, with self-love and altruism. A self-assured, audacious heart is unyielding, making us diligent, wise yet artless, beyond humiliation or fame. A dignified heart respects and cherishes creatures great and small.

A confident and aspiring heart takes wing and reaches for the moon.

The making of a good heart is a long and arduous enterprise, likely a lifelong quest. It is often the hand that rocks the cradle that leaves the early indelible marks on the endeavour. It is an especially noble duty and responsibility of anyone who is to be a parent.

When it is your turn for the making of your heart, you must have a good role model and take great care. Setbacks are inevitable but you can always start again. Never give up and always be vigilant. Heart by nature is intricate and subtle. If you overdo it, its transcendent quality and vigour is gone.

A heart well made is like a ship newly launched. As she is about to set sail for her maiden voyage, the moment, blessed with soaring seagulls under a clear sky, is sacred. A heart of gold radiates goodness even at very low ebb, calling to mind the timbers that make the keel and hulls of a seafaring ship. Should they break into pieces in an unfortunate shipwreck, they could burn brightly, long illuminating the stormy sea.

鱼在波涛下微笑

心在水中。水是什么呢？水就是关系。关系是什么呢？关系就是我们和万物之间密不可分的羁绊。它们如丝如缕百转千回，环绕着我们，滋润着我们，营养着我们，推动着我们；同时，也制约着我们，捆绑着我们，束缚着我们，缠绕着我们。水太少了，心灵就会成为酷日下的撒哈拉。水太多了，堤坝溃塌，如同二〇〇五年夏的新奥尔良，心也会淹得两眼翻白。

人生所有的问题，都是关系的问题。在所有的关系之中，你和你自己的关系最为重要。它是关系的总脐带。如果你处理不好和自我的关系，你的一生就不得安宁和幸福。你可以成功，但没有快乐。你可以有家庭，但缺乏温暖。你可以有孩子，但他难以交流。你可以姹紫嫣红宾朋满座，但却不曾有高山流水患难之交。

你会大声地埋怨这个世界，殊不知症结就在你自己身上。

你爱自己吗？如果你不爱自己，你怎么有能力去爱他人？爱自己是最简单也是最复杂的事情。它不需要任何成本，却需要一个无畏的灵魂。我们每个人都是不完满的，爱一个不完满的自己是勇敢者的行为。

处理好了和自己的关系，你才有精力和智慧去研究你的人际关系，去和大自然和谐相处。如果你被自己搞得焦头烂额，就像一个五内俱空的病人，哪里还有多余的热血去濡养他人！

在水中自由地遨游，闲暇的时候挣脱一切羁绊，到岸上享受晨风拂面，然后，一个华丽的俯冲，重新潜入关系之水，做一条鱼在波涛下微笑。

As a Duck Takes to Water

What sustains our mental well-being, like water keeps a duck afloat? It is our connections to the world, ever present and ever flowing, connecting us with our fellow humans, wrapping around and nourishing us, inspiring us to go on. Yet, they may also bind and constrain us, pulling us down in messy tangles. Without enough sustenance, our soul may wither as if it were cast in sun-baked Sahara. Too much of it, we risk being overwhelmed, as New Orleans was under water when the 2005 hurricane hit.

All problems in life have something to do with our relationships, the most important of which is the one you have with yourself. It affects how you relate to others. If you are not conformable with yourself, you will not have peace and happiness in life. You may be successful, yet deprived of joy. You may start a family, but there will be a lack of warmth. You may have children, yet find communicating with them truly trying. You may live like a swell and be surrounded by an eminent consort of hangers-on, yet your heart will not be free and unencumbered. You have no noble friends that will pick you up when you fall.

You hold a grudge against the world and loudly grumble, little knowing the fault may well lie with you.

Do you love yourself? If you don't, how can you love others? To love yourself could be the simplest or the toughest thing to do. It will cost nothing but require a truly brave soul. None of us is perfect and there is nothing braver than to accept and love an imperfect self.

Only when you can come to terms with yourself, will you then have the strength and wisdom to love others and be in harmony with nature. If you cannot stop tearing yourself into shreds, glum like a car wreck, how do you have enough energy and heart to care for others?

Be a free spirit and true to yourself; try to detach yourself, when you can, from the strands of constraints, the doldrums of necessity, and enjoy the morning breeze in the great outdoors. Then you can dive back into the world of connections, with a smile on your face that radiates from within, and with much ease as a duck takes to water.

假若天使到你家

假如天使到了你家，你会要求些什么？要些什么礼物？

其实人们的要求并不复杂。无非是家人的平安和团聚，足够的衣食温饱，然后就是游玩和快乐了，当然，还有创造。

也许有人会说，要这些凡俗的东西多么无趣啊，既然遇到了天使，就应该向他索要更多的金钱和美色……

乍一想，似乎也有道理。千载难逢的机会砸到了你脑袋上，为什么不狮子大张口，让这些平日你艳羡不止的东西多多益善，将自己包围呢？

好吧，就算有这样宽宏大量的小天使，给了你足够的金钱和美女，然后呢？天使飞走了，你还要继续过下去。你不断地消费金钱，快乐却一点点地减少。这是一条古老的法则——当什么东西充斥在我们周围、无穷无尽的时候，我们就飞快地麻木了。你和美貌的女子周旋，却不会得到爱情，因为没有一个有思想、有爱心的女子会爱上一个饭来张口、衣来伸手的酒囊饭袋。

总之，就像空气、水、盐一样，精神的必需品——爱、欢乐和团圆，是非常朴素却须臾不可离开的。

If an Angel Knocks at Your Door

What if an angel comes knocking at your door? What would you ask for? What blessings would you want?

In truth, most of us have simple needs: safety of our loved ones and the togetherness of family, being fed and clad. Next come play and having fun; then, of course, the need to be productive and creative.

How unimaginative it is to wish for only the mundane, some will say. Now that you have an angel at your door, why don't you wish for more, such as greater fortune and beauty … ?

Come to think of it, they seem to have a point. When such a rare opportunity knocks, why not let your imagination soar, besides opening your door? Let yourself be pampered with the things you have secretly wanted — the more the better.

So there you are with all the money and beauties you ever asked for, thanks to the generosity and resourcefulness of the little angel if there could ever be one. Then, the angel would be gone and you would have to carry on. Your joy would diminish by the day, even if you were spending like a sailor on shore leave. True to aged wisdom, you'd become numb sooner or later when you were bombarded by an infinite supply of all that you ever desired. You might dally with every girl that came your way but be never loved. No thoughtful, caring girl would fall for a bum living on the labour and generosity of others.

In short, love, joy and togetherness — all necessities for our soul — are like air, water and salt and, though humble, are what we truly cannot live without.

绿手指

美国某小镇，有一位老奶奶，长着"绿手指"。千万别以为她是个妖怪或有什么特异，这是当地人对好园丁的称赞。

一天，老人在报上看到一条消息，园艺所重金悬赏纯白金盏花。老奶奶想，金盏花除了金色，就是棕色的，白色的，不可思议。不过，我为什么不试试呢？

她对八个儿女讲了，遭到一致反对。大家说，你根本不懂种子遗传学，专家都不能完成的事，你这么大年纪了，怎么可能完成呢？

老奶奶决心一个人干下去。她撒下金盏花的种子，静心侍弄。金盏花开了，全是橘黄色的。老奶奶在中间挑选了一朵颜色稍淡的花，任其自然枯萎，以取得最好的种子，第二年把它们栽种下去。然后，再从花朵中挑选颜色浅淡的种子，栽种……一年又一年，春种秋收循环往复，老奶奶从不沮丧怀疑，一直坚持。儿女远走了，丈夫去世了，生活中发生了很多的事，老奶奶处理完这些事之后，依然满怀信心地栽种金盏花……

二十年过去了。有一天早晨，她来到花园，看到一朵金盏花开得奇特灿烂。它不是近乎白色，也不是很像白色，是如银如雪的纯白。

她把一百粒种子寄给了那家二十年前悬赏的机构。她甚至不知道这则启事是否还有效，在这漫长的岁月里，是否早就有人培育出了纯白金盏花。

等待的日子长达一年，因为人们要用那些种子验证。终于，园艺所所长打电话给老奶奶说，我们看到了你的花，它是雪白的。因为年代久远，奖金不再兑现。您还有什么要求吗？

老奶奶对着听筒小声说，只想问一问，你们可还要黑色的金盏花？我能种出来……

黑色的金盏花至今没开放，因为老奶奶去世了，世人再没有了这种笨笨的坚持。

但愿你我还能长出新的"绿手指"。

Green Thumb

In a small town in America, there was an elderly woman known for her green thumb. Don't be led into thinking this was something weird or supernatural. The English term simply means a knack for making plants grow well.

As the story goes, the granny read in the local paper one day an announcement by a horticulture society. It was offering an award of a tidy sum of money to anyone who could breed an English marigold of creamy white blooms. She knew that marigolds came in colours of yellow or maroon. She had never thought creamy white could be possible. Then, why couldn't she give it a try?

So she told her eight children who however were united against the idea.

"You know so little about plant breeding," "so they reasoned. It's something even horticulturalists haven't been able to do. What makes you think you can? Besides, you are getting on in years ... "

Yet, she was determined and refused to be talked out of it. She put down seeds and waited for them to grow in their own sweet time. The first blooms were all orange. She spotted one of a paler shade and let it wither naturally for best seeds. They were planted in the following spring and the process was repeated for even paler colours. This went on season after season. She never lost hope, despite setbacks. Her children, all grown-up, moved out and then her husband passed away. Getting over all this with grit, she carried on with her backyard endeavour to get the desired strain of marigold.

Two decades had passed before she saw that most brilliant bloom one morning, as she stepped into her garden. It was not somewhat or nearly white, but pure, snowy white.

She put one hundred seeds in an envelope and mailed it to

the horticulture society, not knowing if the offer of twenty years ago still stood or if someone else had since developed the cream-coloured marigold.

The wait was long as it took a year for the people at the society to test the seeds. Finally, she got a call from its chairman.

" Your marigold is in full bloom now. The flowers are indeed snowy white. However, we won't be able to give you the award, as the offer has lapsed after such a long time. Is there anything else we could do for you? "

" Please tell me if you want a black marigold. Maybe I can do that, too..." the old granny spoke softly into the phone.

We are yet to see any black marigold. The old granny passed away and no one has shown the same stubborn persistence.

I pray that you and I may all have the same green thumb.

我在寻找那片野花

　　 位女友，告诉我这样一件事。

　　上小学的时候，班上有个女同学，叫作荞，家境贫寒，是每学期都免交学杂费的。她衣着破烂，夏天总穿短裤，是捡哥哥剩下的。我和她同期加入少先队，那时候，入队仪式很庄重。新发展的同学面向观众，先站成一排，当然脖子上光秃秃的，此刻还未被吸收入组织嘛。然后一排老队员走上来，和非队员一对一地站好。这时响起令人心跳的进行曲，校长或请来的英模，总之是德高望重的长辈，说着"红领巾是红旗的一角，是用烈士的鲜血染成的"等教诲，把一条条新的红领巾发到老队员手中，再由老队员把这一鲜艳的标志物绕到新队员的脖子上，亲手绾好结，然后互敬队礼，宣告大家都是队友了，隆重的仪式才算完成。

新队员的红领巾，是提前交了钱买下的。荞说她没有钱。辅导员说，那怎么办呢？荞说，哥哥已超龄退队，她可用哥哥的旧领巾。于是，那天授红领巾的仪式，就有一点儿特别。当辅导员用托盘把新红领巾呈到领导手中的时候，低低地说了一句。同学们虽听不清是什么，但也能猜出来——那是提醒领导，轮到荞的时候，记得把托盘里的那条旧红领巾分给她。

满盘的新红领巾好似一塘金红的鲤鱼，支棱着翅角。旧红领巾软绵绵地卧着，仿佛混入的灰鲫，落寞孤独。那天来的领导，可能老了，不曾听清这句格外的交代，也许根本没想到还有这等复杂的事。总之，他一一发放红领巾，走到荞的面前，随手把一条新红领巾分给了她。我看到荞好像被人砸了一下头顶，身体矮了下去，灿如火苗的红领巾环着她的脖子，也无法映暖她苍白的脸庞。

那个交了新红领巾的钱，却分到一条旧红领巾的女孩，委屈至极。她当场不好发作，刚一散会，就怒气冲冲地跑到荞跟前，一把扯住荞的红领巾说，这是我的！你还给我！

红领巾是一个活结，被女孩拽住一股猛拉就系死了，好似一条绞索，把荞勒得眼珠凸起，喘不过气来。

大伙扑上去拉开她俩。荞满眼都是泪花，窒得直咳嗽。

那个抢红领巾的女孩自知理亏，嘟囔着，本来就是我的嘛！谁要你的破红领巾！说着，女孩把荞哥哥的旧红领巾一把扯下，丢到荞的身上，补了一句——我们的红领巾都是烈士用鲜血染的，你的这条红色这么淡，是用刷牙刷出的血染的。

经她这么一说，我们更觉得荞的那条旧得凄凉。风雨洗过，阳光晒过，褪了颜色，布丝已褪为浅粉；铺在脖子后方的三角顶端部分，几乎成了白色；耷拉在胸前的两个角，因为摩挲和洗涤，絮毛纷披，好似炸开的锅刷头。

我们都为荞鸣不平，觉得那女孩太霸道了。荞却一声未吭，把新红领巾折得齐整整，还了它的主人；又把旧红领巾端端系好，默默地走了。

后来我问荞，她那样对你，你就不伤心吗？荞说，谁都想要新红领巾啊，我能想通。只是她说我的红领巾是用刷牙刷出的血染的，我不服。我的红领巾原来也是鲜红的，哥哥从九岁戴到十五岁，时间很久了。真正的血，也会褪色的。我试过了。

我吓了一跳。心想，她该不是自己挤出一点儿血，涂在布上，做过什么试验吧？我没敢问，怕得到一个肯定的答复。

毕业的时候，荞的成绩很好，可以上重点中学，但因为家境艰难，只考了一所技工学校，以期早早分担父母的窘困。

在现今的社会里，如果没有意外的变故，接受良好的教育，是从较低阶层进入较高阶层的，不说是唯一，也是最基本的孔道。荞在很小的时候，就放弃了这种可能。她也不是国色天香的女孩，没有王子骑了白马来会她。所以，荞以后的路，就一直在贫困的底层挣扎。

我们这些同学，已接近了知天命的岁月。在经历了种种的人生，尘埃落定之后，屡屡举行聚会，忆旧兼互通联络。荞很少参加，只说是忙。于是，那个当年扯她红领巾的女子说，荞可能是混得不如人，不好意思见老同学了。

荞是一家印刷厂的女工。早几年，厂子还开工时，她送过我一本交通地图。说是厂里总是印账簿一类的东西，一般人用不上的，碰上一回印地图，她赶紧给我留了一册，想我有时外出或许会用得着。

说真的，正因为常常外出，各式地图我很齐备，但我还是非常高兴地收下了她的馈赠。我知道，这是她能拿得出的最好的礼物了。

一次聚会，荞终于来了。她所在的工厂宣布破产，她成了下岗女工。她的丈夫出了车祸，抢救后性命虽无碍，但伤了腿，从此吃不得重力。儿子得了肝炎休学，需要静养和高蛋白。她在几个地方连做小时工，十分奔波辛苦。这次刚好到这边打工，于是抽空和老同学见见面。

我们都不知说什么好，只是紧握着她的手。她的掌上有很多毛刺，好像一把尼龙丝板刷。

半小时后，荞要走了。同学们推我送送她。我打了一辆车，送她去干活的地方。本想在车上多问问她的近况，又怕伤了她的尊严，正斟酌为难时，她突然叫起来——你看！你快看！

窗外是城乡接合部的建筑工地，尘土纷扬，杂草丛生，毫无风景。我不解地问，你要我看什么呢？

荞很开心地说，我要你看路边的那一片野花啊。每天我从这里过的时候，都要寻找它们。我知道它们哪天张开叶子，哪天抽出花茎，哪天早晨突然就开了……我每天都向它们问好呢！

我一眼看去，野花已风驰电掣地闪走了，不知是橙是蓝，看到的只是荞的脸，憔悴之中有了花一样的神采。于是，我那颗久久悬起的心，稳稳地落下了。我不再问她任何具体的事情，彼此已是相知。人的一生，谁知有多少艰涩在等着我们？但荞经历了重重风雨之后，还在寻找一片不知名的野花，问候着它们。我知道在她心中，还贮备着丰足的力量和充沛的爱，足以抵抗征程的霜雪和苦难。

此后，我外出的时候，总带着荞送我的地图册。

朋友这样结束了她的故事。

Looking for that Patch of Wildflowers

A friend of mine told me this story:

In primary school, I had a classmate. Her name was Qiao. Her family was poor, so the school waived her tuitions every year. She was always in ragged clothing. In summer, she would wear short pants that were hand-me-downs from her elder brother. We joined the Young Pioneers in the batch, which in our time always meant a solemn induction ceremony. The new recruits stood shoulder to shoulder in front of the school assembly, ready to be inducted. A crimson kerchief, the token of Young Pioneer membership, would be tied around each of their necks till then looking rather bare. A covey of current members would walk up and stand in front of the neophytes. To the rousing tune of a march, a revered elder — a model worker, a decorated veteran, or the school principal himself — would hand out the bright red kerchiefs one by one to the current members, after reading from a note proclaiming "the scarf represents the missing triangle on the Young Pioneer flag and its red colour comes from the blood of martyrs of the Revolution." The current members would turn around and wrap a kerchief around each neophyte's neck with an elaborate knot. This would be followed by an exchange of the Pioneer's salute, signifying they were all fellow Young Pioneers now and bringing the solemn proceedings to an end.

Everyone had to pay for their new neckerchiefs beforehand. Qiao didn't have the money. She said she could use her brother's hand-me-down instead when asked by the school counsellor. So, the pupils assembled that day saw something odd: when passing the tray of neckerchiefs to the guest of honour, the counsellor apparently said something to him. Though nobody could make out what that was, they guessed it was to remind him for whom the worn-out neckerchief was intended.

The new kerchiefs, bright red and crisp with tilting corners, lay in the tray like folded paper goldfish. The faded, worn neckerchief stood out, like the lone mutant in a pond of red goldfish. The elderly guest of honour apparently missed his cue. He hadn't expected the gig to involve such intricacy. As he passed out the scarves one after another, a new one was handed to Qiao. For an instant, Qiao recoiled as if she had been whacked over the head, her face pale in the glow of the flaming red new scarf.

The girl who was given the old scarf looked hurt. Having managed to keep the lid on during the ceremony, she accosted Qiao right afterwards. Grabbing Qiao by the scarf, she exploded, "This is mine! Give it back!"

Tied in a slipknot, the neckerchief tightened

like a noose. Qiao almost choked, her eyes bulging out.

Others rushed over to pull them apart. Qiao, her eyes brimming with tears, was seized with a coughing fit.

Realizing now she was in the wrong, the girl whimpered, "That should have been mine. Who wants this old rag?!" She tore Qiao's brother's old scarf off her neck and threw it back at Qiao, adding, "The red of Young Pioneer's scarf comes from martyrs' blood, but yours is so pale! It must have come from the rinse after brushing your gums."

At this, we all felt even more pitiful for the old scarf. Worse for wear and bleached by exposure to sunlight, it was threadbare at the corners and its colour barely pink. The obtuse angle that draped behind the neck was washed grey and the two front angles frayed and threadbare.

We took up for Qiao; all feeling the girl was a bully. However, Qiao kept silent. She neatly folded the new scarf before giving it back to its owner. She then put on the worn scarf with a neat knot and quietly walked off.

"Weren't you sad when she did that to you? " I asked Qiao

later.

"She could understand," Qiao said. "Nobody wants an old scarf. What I couldn't swallow was her saying the old scarf being dyed with the rinse from tooth brushing. The old scarf was once bright red, too. My brother had worn it from age nine till he was fifteen. Even real blood would have faded over time. I knew because I had tested it."

This gave me a little shock. Could she really have pricked herself and test the blood on a piece of cloth? I didn't ask, fearing I might get a confirmation.

Soon it was school graduation. With the grades she got, Qiao could have gone on to a "key" high school (with the promise of college). However, because of her family's threadbare existence, she chose vocational college instead, hoping to help improve their meagre lot by getting into the workforce earlier.

In our culture, education is seen as the main,

if not the only, path to a higher social station, barring the unexpected. Qiao had given up such a possibility when she was so young. She was by no means endowed with out-of-this-world kind of beauty, such that a regular Prince Charming would trot her way. Thus, she has led a lowly existence, barely scraping by ever since.

By now, my schoolmates have all reached a point in life where our years of strife are behind us. We began to often wax the philosophical and were eager to have school reunions from time to time; to reconnect and reminisce. Yet, Qiao rarely showed up, giving the excuse of being busy. To this, the girl who had grabbed Qiao's scarf would say, "Perhaps she is not doing well in life, so she shied away from seeing old schoolmates."

Qiao had worked at a printing plant. Years ago, when the factory was still in operation, she gave me a road atlas, saying that I might find it handy when I went on occasional trips. She added that she had kept one for me when the factory took that rare job of printing atlases, as usually all it printed were all ledgers and the like, which most people wouldn't have any use for.

As I do travel quite often, I have kept a good collection of maps of all sorts. Still, I was most happy to have this one from her, for I knew it was probably the best she could do when it came to giving someone a gift.

At last, she showed up at one reunion. The factory she had worked for closed down and she lost her job. Then her husband was injured in a road accident. Though he recovered from his serious injuries, he couldn't lift anything heavy due to permanent damage to one of his legs. Her son had hepatitis and had to stay at home and keep to a high protein diet. So she took up several part-time jobs, rushing from one to next. It happened that the reunion party was near one of her jobs. So she came by to see her alumni.

Everyone struggled to find the right thing to say and ended up greeting her by squeezing her hand. Her callous hand felt rough, like a brush of tough, short bristles.

She stayed for only half an hour. Everyone said I should walk with her and see her off. I flagged down a cab and planned to drop her off at her next job. I hesitated to ask how she was doing, fearing it might hurt her. As I was debating with myself, she shouted excitedly, "Look! Quick! There it is!"

Through the windows of the cab, I saw a construction site in some urban boundary area, dusty and overgrown with weed. I was puzzled, "What do you want me to see?"

"I want you to look at that patch of wildflowers. I would look for them as I passed here every day. I know when the new leaves sprouted, when the buds started showing, and when they burst into bloom on one of those mornings. They greeted me every day!" Qiao said ebulliently.

As I turned to look, the wildflowers had flashed past in a blur. Are they orange or blue? I wasn't sure. However, what I saw clearly was Qiao's face, which, although toil-worn, took on a glow; like that of flowers in full bloom. My heart that had ached for her now felt light. I already knew how her life had been, without having to get every last detail, as if we had known each other all along. The trials we all had been through in our lives were beyond telling. Qiao had weathered it all in stride and she was still looking out for that wild patch of unknown flowers, greeting them every day. I knew at that instant she had an ample store of strength and love deep within, enough to see her through life's many adversities.

From then on, I would never go on a journey without the atlas she had given me.

So ends the remarkable story my friend told me.

爱怕什么

爱挺娇气挺笨挺糊涂的，有很多怕的东西。

爱怕撒谎。当我们不爱的时候，假装爱，是一件痛苦而倒霉的事情。假如别人识破，我们就成了虚伪的坏蛋。你骗了别人的钱，可以退赔；你骗了别人的爱，就成了无赦的罪人。假如别人不曾识破，那就更惨。除非你已良心丧尽，否则便要承诺爱的假象，那心灵深处的绞杀，永无宁日。

爱怕沉默。太多的人，以为爱到深处是无言。其实爱是很难描述的一种感情，需要详尽的表达和传递。爱需要行动，但爱绝不仅仅是行动，或者说语言和温情的流露，也是行动不可或缺的部分。我曾经和朋友们做过一个测验，让一个人心中充满一种独特的感觉，然后用表情和手势做出来，让其他不知底细的人猜测他的内心活动。出谜和解谜的人都欣然答应，自以为万无一失。结果，能正确解码的人少得可怜。当你自觉满脸爱意的时候，他人误读的结论千奇百怪。比如认为那是——矜持、发呆、忧郁……

一位妈妈胸有成竹地低下头，做出一个表情。我和另一位女士愣愣地看着她，相互对视了一下，异口同声地说，你要自杀！她愤怒地瞪着我们说，岂有此理！你们怎那么笨？我此刻心头正充盈温情！愚笨的我俩挺惭愧的，但没等我们道歉的话出口，那妈妈恍然大悟道，原来是这样！怪不得我每次这样看着儿子的时候，他会不安地说：妈妈，我又做错了什么？你又在发什么愁？

爱是那样地需要表达，就像耗竭太快的电器，每日都得充电。重复而新鲜地描述爱意吧，它是一种勇敢和智慧的艺术。

爱怕犹豫。爱是羞怯和机灵的，一不留神它就吃了鱼饵闪去。爱的初起往往是柔弱无骨的碰撞和翩若惊鸿的引力。在爱的极早期，就敏锐地识别自己的真爱，是一种能力，更是一种果敢。爱一桩事业，就奋不顾身地投入。爱一种信仰，就至死不悔。

爱怕模棱两可。要么爱这一个，要么爱那一个，遵循一种

"全或无"的铁则。爱，就铺天盖地，不遗下一个角落。不爱就抽刀断水，金盆洗手。迟疑延宕是对他人和自己的不负责任。

爱怕沙上建塔。那样的爱，无论多么玲珑剔透，潮起潮落，遗下的只是无珠的蚌壳和断根的水草。

爱怕无源之水。沙漠里的河啊，即便不是海市蜃楼，波光粼粼又能坚持几天？当沙暴袭来的时候，最先干涸的正是泪水积聚的咸水湖。

爱怕假冒伪劣。真的爱也许不那么外表光滑、色彩艳丽，没有精致的包装，没有夸口的广告，但它有内在的质量保证。真爱并非不会发生短路与损伤，但是它有保修单，那是两颗心的承诺，写在天地间。

爱是一个有机整体，怕分割。好似钢化玻璃，据说坦克压上也不会碎，可惜它的弱点是宁折不弯，脆不可裁。一旦破碎，就裂成了无数蚕豆大的渣滓，流淌一地，闪着凄楚的冷光，再也无法复原。

爱的脚力不健，怕远。距离会漂白彼此相思的颜色，假如有可能，就靠得近一点，再近一点，直到水乳交融亲密无间。万万不要人为地以分离考验它的强度，那你也许会后悔莫及。尽量地创造并肩携手天人合一的时光。

爱像仙人掌类的花朵，怕转瞬即逝。爱可以不朝朝暮暮，爱可以不卿卿我我，但爱要铁杵磨成针，恒远久长。

爱怕平分秋色。在爱的钢丝上不能学高空王子，不宜做危险动作。即使你摇摇晃晃，一时不曾跌落，也是偶然性在救你，任何一阵旋风，都可能使你飘然坠毁。最明智最保险的是赶快从高空回到平地，在泥土上留下深深脚印。

爱怕刻意求工。爱可以披头散发，爱可以荆钗布裙，爱可以粗茶淡饭，爱可以风餐露宿。只要一腔真情，爱就有了依傍。

爱的时候，眼睛近视散光，只爱看江山如画；耳是聋的，只爱听莺歌燕语。爱让人片面，爱让人轻信。爱让人智商下降，爱让人一厢情愿。爱最怕的，是腐败。爱需要天天注入激情的活力，但又如深潭，波澜不惊。

说了爱的这许多毛病，爱岂不一无是处？

爱是世上最坚固的记忆金属，高温下不熔化，冰冻不脆裂。造一架爱的航天飞机，你就可以驾驶着它，遨游九天。

爱是比天空和海洋更博大的宇宙，在那个独特的穹隆中，有着亿万颗爱的星斗，闪烁光芒。一粒小行星划下，就是爱的雨丝，缀起满天清光。

爱是神奇的化学试剂，能让苦难变得香甜，能让一分钟驻成永远，能让平凡的容颜貌若天仙，能让喃喃细语压过雷鸣电闪。

爱是孕育万物的草原。在这里，能生长出能力、勇气、智慧、才干、友谊、关怀……所有人间的美德和属于大自然的美丽天分，爱都会赠予你。

在生和死之间，是孤独的人生旅程。保有一份真爱，就是照耀人类得以温暖的灯。

What Affects Love?

Love is delicate, innocent and gullible. It is affected by many things.

Love fears lying. To pretend to be in love when we are not is unfortunate and painful. People eventually see through your deceit. Should you cheat others out of their money, you might mend by giving it all back. Yet if you cheat in a relationship, you are an irredeemable criminal. It is actually even worse if you haven't been caught with your hand in the till. Your pretending will begin to eat away at what is left of your conscience, tormenting you without respite.

Love fears silence. Most of us think the deepest love is

beyond words. Indeed, love is a feeling that is difficult to articulate in words; yet it needs to be expressed and conveyed fully. Love demands action, yet actions alone are not enough. Rather, words and expressions of tenderness are indispensable in deeds of love. I once did an experiment with a few friends. One person was to call up a unique feeling and then act it using facial expressions and gestures, while others guessed what that feeling was. When they were given the rules, everyone was game and thought they could breeze through it. As it turned out, few could decipher all the gesticulation and expressions. When one person was acting being affectionate, others' reading was rich — aloof, dazed, even depressed ...

A young mother lowered her head and put on a deliberate expression, seemingly knowing what she was doing. Another woman and I stared at her, exchanged a look and then said in unison, "You are suicidal!" She met our remark with a scowl, "Nonsense! How could you so be dumb? I was glowing with affection!" Looking stupid, we felt very sorry. Before we could apologize, the young mother suddenly divined, "Gosh. That's what then. No wonder every time I looked at my son this way, he would ask with unease: 'What did I do wrong? Why are you sad, mum?'"

Love needs to be expressed effectively, just as an electronic device needs daily recharging lest it be depleted of power. Express love; repeat it often in a refreshing manner. It is an art that demands courage and wisdom of its practitioner.

Love shuns hesitation. Love is shy and ethereal. It is the fish that niggles at the bait and is gone just as you let your guard down. Love often begins with tentative overtures, a sense of elusive chemistry and fleeting gravitation. Recognizing one's true love in life early on is not only a knack but also unflinching courage. You are all in when doing what you love and unwavering on the path of faith till the very end.

Love fears duplicity. You love totally either this or that, abiding by the principle of "all or none." Love fills all. When love is lost, throw in the towel and let go. Don't dither or linger, for this is the only responsible thing you can do to others and yourself.

Love has no room for vanity. Vanity is all gloss and varnish, like an oyster without grit producing no pearls, or seaweeds with holdfasts cut withering in the ebb and flow.

Love is doomed without a wellspring deep within. A desert stream, if it is not a mirage, soon ceases to flow without a wellspring. A small waterhole, mere teardrops in a vast desert, dries up the quickest when a sandstorm hits.

Love also fears pretension and falsification. True love flows from deep within, unadorned and lacking resplendent colours. It needs no fancy packaging or boastful broadcasting. It is something of superior quality and, though not immune to short-circuiting or malfunction, is guaranteed by the mutual commitment of two people, with the power of the heart above all else.

Love is whole, adverse to division. It can endure immense force, like tempered glass, capable of standing even the weight of an army tank, so it was said. Yet with no elasticity, it would break rather than bend when the force exceeds the limit of its endurance. When broken, it splits into thumb-sized pieces, roundish and shattered beyond amend, like a thousand forlorn eyes.

Love fears separation. Great distances may bleach its intense hues. Shorten the distance; get closer until you know not where one ends and another begins. Never try to test your resilience to separation; you will regret so. Try as you can to be close to each other, hand in hand and shoulder to shoulder, in heavenly harmony as the creator has intended since the beginning of time.

Love should not be ephemeral, like the short-lived cactus blossoms that are there and gone before the day is over. Love may not be all bill and coo. The bond of love should only grow all the stronger over time, through thick and thin.

Love with a divided heart is akin to tightrope walking. You should never attempt such a tricky act, for you will be doomed, even though you might have momentary success thanks to chance. It is wisest to get down from that perilous perch and put your feet firmly on the solid ground.

Love is artless, undiminished by the lacking of decorum or the finer things in life. Love can thrive in a life of simplicity, impervious to harsh conditions and living with the bare minimum. If you give each other your heart, that is a solid foundation of love.

Love can be nearsighted, seeing only beauty in the landscape. Love fools our ears, blotting out all but the sweetest song. We become partial and gullible when we are in love. It lowers our IQ and traps us in wishful thinking. Love is adverse to stagnation and decay, needing daily invigoration. It can also be tranquil, like still waters that run deep.

Given all that is negative, isn't love by and

large fickle?

Yet, love is also most resilient, like the toughest shape-memory alloy, and stable at extreme temperatures. Love should be like such superior metal, unbreakable. Let love soar, like a voyager constructed with high-performance materials, on an amazing journey into the boundless space.

Love is the universe, immense beyond all else. Yet its unfathomable depth is filled with stars in their multitudes, each blazingly glorious. From time to time, a shooting star glides across, like drizzle of love.

Love is the magic spell that turns a harsh life sweet, the momentary eternal, the plain glorious, and the small voices thunderous.

Love is the grassland that has nourished creatures great and small. Love is the wellspring of our strength, courage, wisdom, ability, affection, and compassion. All the human goodness and beauty endowed by nature, love will bestow on you.

On the lonely journeys between life and death, true love, dearly held, is the blazing light that warms humanity's heart.

教养的证据

教养是个高频词。时下，如果说某人没教养，就是大批评大贬义了。

什么叫教养呢？

词典上说是"文化和品德的修养"，但我更愿意理解为"因教育而养成的优良品质和习惯"。

一个人受过教育，但他依然有可能是没有教养的。就像一个人不停地吃东西，但他的肠胃不吸收，竹篮打水一场空，还是骨瘦如柴。不过这话似乎不能反过来说——一个人没有受过系统的教育，他却能够很有教养。

教养不是天生的。一个小孩子如果没有人教给他良好的习惯和有关的知识，他必定是愚昧和粗浅的。当然，这个"教"是广义的，除了指入学经师，也包括家长的言传身教和对环境的耳濡目染。

教养和财富一样，是需要证据的。你说你有钱不成，得拿出一个资产证明。教养的证据不是你读过多少书，家庭背景如何显赫，也不是你通晓多少礼节规范，能够熟练使用刀叉，会穿晚礼服……这些仅仅是一些表面的气泡，最关键的证据可能有如下若干。

热爱大自然。把它列为有教养的证据之首，是因为一个不懂得敬畏大自然，不知道人类渺小的人，必是井底之蛙，与教养谬之千里。这也许怪不得他，因为如果不经教育，一个人是很难自发地懂得宇宙之大和人类的微小的。没有相应的自然科学知识，人除了显得蒙昧和狭隘以外，注定也是盲目傲慢的。之所以从小就教育孩子要爱护花草，正是对这种伟大感悟的最基本的训练。若是看到一个成人野蛮地攀折林木，通常人们就会毫不迟疑地评判道——这个人太没有教养了。可见，教养和绿色是紧密地联系在一起的。懂得与自然协调相处，懂得爱护无言的植物的人，推而广之，他多半也可能会爱惜更多的动物，爱护自己的同类。

一个有教养的人，应该能够自如地运用公共的语言，表达自己的内心和同他人交流，并能妥帖地付诸文字。我所说的公共语言，是指大家——从普通民众到知识分子都能理解的清洁和明亮的语言，而不是某种受众面狭窄的土语俚语或者某特定情境下的专业语言。这个要求并非画蛇添足。在这个千帆竞发的时代，太多的人，只会说他那个行业的内部语言，只会说机器仪器能听懂的语言，却不懂得和人亲密地交流。这不是一个批评，而是一个事实。和人交流的掌握，特别是和陌生人的沟通，通常不是自发产生的，是要通过学习和练习来获得的。一个没有受过教育的人，他所掌握的词汇是有限和贫乏的，除了描绘自己的生理感受，比如饿了、渴了、睡觉之外，他对于自己的内心感知甚为模糊。因为那些描述内心感受的词汇，通常是抽象和长于比兴的，不通过学习，难以明确恰当地将它表达出来。那些虽然拥有一技之长，但无法精彩地运用公共语言这种神圣的媒介来沟通和解读自我心灵的人，难以算是一个有教养的人。技术是用来谋生的，而仅仅具有谋生的本领是不够的。就像豺狼也会自发地猎取食物一样，那是近乎无须教育也可掌握的本能。而人，毫无疑问地应比豺狼更高一筹。

一个有教养的人，对历史应有恰如其分的了解，知道生而为人，我们走过了怎样曲折的道路。当然，教养并不能使每个人都像历史学家那样博古通今，但是教养却能使一个有思考爱好的人，知晓我们是从哪里来，要到哪里去。教养通过历史，使我们不单活在此时此刻，也活在从前和以后，如同生活在一条奔腾的大河里，知道泉眼和海洋的方向。

　　一个有教养的人，除了眼前的事物和得失以外，他还会不由自主地想到他远大的目标。教养把人的注意力拓展了，变得宏大和光明。每一个个体都有沉没在黑暗峡谷的时刻，跋涉和攀缘其中，虽然伤痕累累，因为你具有的教养，确知时间是流动的，明了暂时与永久，相信在遥远的地方，定有峡谷的出口，那里有瀑布在轰鸣。

　　一个有教养的人，对自己的身体，要有亲切的了解和珍惜之情。知道它们各自独有的清晰的名称，明了它们是精致和洁净的，身体的每一部分都有着不可替代的功能，并无高低贵贱的区别。他知道自己的快乐和满足，有很大一部分是建筑在这些功能的灵敏和感知的健全上的。他也毫无疑义地知道，他的大脑是他的身体的主宰。他不会任由他的器官牵制他的所作所为，他是清醒和有驾驭力的。他在尊重自己身体的同时，也尊重他人的身体；在尊重自我的权利的同时，也尊重他人的权利；在驰骋自我意志的骏马时，也精心维护着他人的茵茵草地。

一个有教养的人，对人类种种优秀的品质，比如忠诚、勇敢、信任、勤勉、互助、舍己救人、临危不惧、吃苦耐劳、坚贞不屈……应充满敬重、敬畏、敬仰之心。不一定每一个人都能够身体力行，但他们懂得爱戴和歌颂。人不是不可以怯懦和懒惰，但他不能把这些陋习伪装成高风亮节，不能由于自己做不到高尚，就诋毁所有做到了这些的人是伪善。你可以跪在泥里，但你不可以把污泥抹上整个世界的胸膛，并因此煞有介事地说到处都是污垢。

一个有教养的人，知道害怕。知道害怕是件有意义、有价值的事情。它表示明了自己的限制，知道世上有一些不可逾越的界限。知道世界上有阳光，阳光下有正义的惩罚。由于害怕正义的惩罚，因而约束自我，是意志力坚强的一种体现。

一个有教养的人，知道仰视高山和宇宙，知道仰视那些伟大的发现和人格，知道对于自己无法企及的高度表达尊重，而不是糊涂地闭上眼睛或是居心叵测地嘲讽。

教养是不可一蹴而就的。教养是细水长流的。

教养是可以遗失也可以捡拾起来的。教养也具有某种坚定的流传性和既定的轨道性。教养是一些习惯的总和，在某种程度上，教养不是活在我们的皮肤上，是繁衍在我们的骨髓里。教养和遗传几乎是不相关的，是后天和社会的产物。教养必须要有酵母，在潜移默化和条件反射的共同烘烤下，假以足够的时日，才能自然而然地散发出香气。

　　教养是衡量一个民族整体素质的一张X光片。脸面上可以依靠化妆繁花似锦，但只有内在的健硕，才经得起冲刷和考验，才是力量的象征。

Proper Upbringing

Upbringing has become an oft-repeated word. Saying someone has not been properly brought up is of late an utmost expression of contempt and scorn.

But what does upbringing mean?

The dictionary suggests "cultural sophistication and cultivated moral character." However, I would rather see it as "fine attributes and habit acquired through education."

A person may be educated, yet remains lacking in character, just as he may gorge on food, but is scrawny, even all skin and bones, thanks to indigestion that renders his eating vain. However, the reverse — that a person lacking systematic education can have a fine character — is not likely to be true.

One is not born to have a fine character. A child, if he is not educated to develop a sound habit and acquire knowledge, will grow up shallow and ignorant. The word "educated," of course, was used in its broadest sense, including parents' teaching and role-modelling, and environmental influences, as well as schooling.

Proper upbringing has telling signs, like a certain certificate of assets that proves your worth. The proof of proper upbringing lies not in how many books you have read, how powerful your family's connections are, how well you are versed in etiquette — picking the right evening dress or formal attire; knowing the right way of using the cutlery — which are nothing but trivial and superfluous. The signs of the well-brought-up are in a class of their own.

The first of these is a love of nature. A man who has no reverence for nature and knows not the cosmic insignificance of humanity is like the frog in a well that knows nothing of the great ocean. When it comes to being properly brought up, he might the very one. Without learning, a man is not likely to comprehend by intuition how mind-bogglingly big the universe is and how infinitely small human beings are. Without knowledge of natural science, one is prone to being ignorant and puffed up, besides looking dim and narrow. That's why parents urge children to observe plants and flowers, so that through such basic training they gain a great sense of reverence for nature. If a grown man is seen savagely causing damage to trees and plants, he will instantly be judged by others as lacking proper upbringing. It goes to show that cultivation is somehow linked with the world of the living green. One who knows the importance of being in harmony with nature, and cares about trees and plants, would most likely project such compassion to all living creatures and his fellow humans.

A man properly brought up should be able to

comfortably express himself and communicate with others, using the common language with ease, both verbally and in proper writing. By the word "common", I meant clear and effective language accessible to all — from the man in the street to the highly educated — as opposed to vernacular talk or professional jargon suited for limited contexts. This is not an idle request; frivolous as painting the lily. In this day and age, with new paths being broken and new specializations multiplying by the minute, many talks in jargons understandable only to the initiated. They are versed in languages that are meaningful to machines, but incapable of speaking with clarity and feeling to fellow humans. I say this not as a criticism, but as a fact. The skills for effectively communicating with others, especially those you do not know well, are to be acquired through learning and practice, rather than something you are born with. An uneducated person has a limited and pale vocabulary. He finds it hard to clearly describe feelings and emotions, beyond what is physiological, such as hunger, thirst, and sleepiness. Words for innermost feelings are often abstract and best rendered in figures of speech; a knack mastered through learning. Those who have specialized knowledge but can't articulate their innermost feelings, in common yet splendid language, cannot really be counted as having had a proper upbringing. Technical expertise is used to make a living, which alone is not enough. Predatory beasts, with skills acquired instinctively, are masters of preying. Human beings, no doubt, have to be a cut above that.

A person properly brought up should also have a proper sense of history, knowing what arduous journey humanity has taken and how we have arrived at where we are. Needless to say, proper upbringing does not necessarily make everyone an all-knowing historian. Yet it does allow the most curious and pensive of us to learn where we have come from and where we are headed. It allows us to live not merely in the present, but also in the past and future, connected as if by a river rushing from the headwater to reach the vast ocean.

A man properly brought up cannot help thinking the long-term. He never loses sight of his ambitious goal, beyond his present preoccupation and petty calculation. Education broadens our mind and makes us generous and sunny. We may all have stumbled, at one time or another on our life's journey, into a deep, dark ravine. Yet we were able to remain unruffled and optimistic thanks to our upbringing. We know full well, despite the brutal trek and getting bruised all over, that time does not stand still, winds change, and, no matter how distant, there is an opening at the end of the hemmed-in ravine; airily bright and roaring with a waterfall.

Indeed, the well-brought-up should also have a thorough knowledge of his body and know how to care for it. Each and every organ, miracles of creation, should be clean and properly named. They are all indispensable and none is inferior. He knows that his sense of wellbeing and happiness depends in large measure on their flawless functioning and healthy sensory impressions. He also knows without a doubt his body is subject to the control of his mind. He is sober and in command and wouldn't stand the nonsense of his bodily parts getting the upper hand. He respects his own body as well as that of another, just as he equally respects his own rights and those of others, never trespassing on another's pasture while roaming wild and free.

A person, properly brought up, regards all of the fine human qualities — being loyal, audacious, trusting, diligent, generous, altruistic, fearless in the face of danger, forbearing and unyielding — with respect, reverence and admiration. He keenly appreciates and applauds such great qualities, though he may not be able to emulate them all. Granted that humans can be timid, meek and slothful, these flawed traits should not be elevated as simplicity and artlessness. He who fails to attain the fine qualities should not attack those who do as being pretentious. He may walk on his knees in the muck for all we care, but he is none to sling mud at others or accuse everyone else of being crooked.

The well-bred maintains a certain sense of apprehension. This is something of value and significance, as it reflects an awareness of limits and boundaries. As he believes all evils under the sun shall be punished in the interest of justice. He melts his self-discipline and the fear of punishment into a moral strength.

The well-brought-up senses the immenseness of majestic mountains and the boundless universe. He is awed by the great discoveries and noble human character and respects human attainment yet beyond his reach. He never turns his back on such attainment or treats it with vicious scorn.

A fine character is built over time; never overnight. It may be lost and reinstated. It can be enduring and infectious and has a trajectory of its own. It is the sum of behaviours — an outward expression of the character that is deep-seated and permeates the core of our being. It is not something in the genes but carries the imprint of family and society. It is shaped through moulding and conditioning over time, very much like leavening, baking and time eventually giving rise to that delightful aroma of the baked bread.

An individual's upbringing is also a reflection, each and collectively, of the national character. It is the innate strength of a nation, capable of standing the test of time and trials of hardships; a sign of its health beyond the hurly-burly and mere cosmetic rosiness.

友谊这棵树上的果子

现代人的友谊，很坚固又很脆弱。它是人间的宝藏，我们须珍爱。友谊的不可传递性，决定了它是一部孤本的书。我们可以和不同的人有不同的友谊，但我们不会和同一个人有不同的友谊。友谊是一条越拥越深的巷道，没有回头路可以走，刻骨铭心的友谊也如仇恨一样，没齿难忘。

友情这棵树上只结一个果子，叫作信任。红苹果只留给灌溉果树的人品尝。别的人摘下来尝一口，很可能酸倒了牙。

友谊之链不可继承，不可转让，不可贴上封条保存起来而不腐烂，不可冷冻在冰箱里永远新鲜。

友谊需要滋养。有的人用钱，有的人用汗，还有的人用血。友谊是很贪婪的，绝不会满足于餐风饮露。友谊是最简朴同时也是最奢侈的营养，需要用时间去灌溉。友谊必须述说，友谊必须倾听，友谊必须交谈的时刻双目凝视，友谊必须倾听的时分全神贯注。友谊有的时候是那样脆弱，一句不经意的言辞，就会使大厦顷刻倒塌。友谊有的时候是那样容易变质，一个未经证实的传言就会让整盆牛奶变酸。这个世界日新月异。在什么都是越现代越好的年代里，唯有友谊，人们保持着古老的准则：朋友就像文物，越老越珍贵。

礼物分两种，一种是实用的，一种是象征性的。

我喜欢送实用的礼物。

不单是因为它可为朋友提供立等可取的服务功能，更因为我的利己考虑。

此刻我们是朋友，十年以后不一定是朋友。

就算你耿耿忠心，对方也许早已淡忘。

速朽的礼物，既表达了我此时此刻的善意，又给予朋友可果腹、可悦目、可哈哈一笑或是凝神端详的价值，虽是一次性的，也留下美好的瞬间，我心足矣。象征久远意义的礼物，若是人家不珍惜这份友谊了，留着就是尴尬，或丢或毁，都是物件的悲哀，我的心在远处也会颤抖。

若是给自己的礼物，还是具有象征意义的好。比如，一块石头、一片树叶，在别人眼里那样普通，其中的美妙含义只有自己知晓。

电话簿是一只储存朋友的魔盒，假如我遇到困难，就要向他们发出求救信号。一种畏惧孤独的潜意识，像冬眠的虫子蛰伏在心灵的旮旯儿。人生一世，消失的是岁月，收获的是朋友。虽然我有时会几天不同任何朋友联络，但我知道自己牢牢地黏附于友谊网络之中。

利害关系这件事，实在是交友的大敌。我不相信有永久的利益，我更珍视患难与共的友谊。长留史册的，不是锱铢必较的利益，而是肝胆相照的情分，和朋友坦诚地交往，会使我们留存对真情的敏感，会使我的眼睛抹去云翳，心境重新开朗。

Tree of Friendship

Friendship in modern society can be enduring, yet fragile. Friendship is truly life's treasure to be dearly cherished. Friendship is not transferable, each unique like a rare book. We may have different friendships with different people, yet never different friendships with the same person. It is a one-directional path that extends as friendship deepens and allows no turning back. A friendship that touches our heart and soul marks our life deeply, indelible like hatred to the end.

The tree of friendship bears only one fruit — trust. Red as apple, it is reserved for the one who tends to the tree. Anyone else picking and taking a bite of it will find it sour as vinegar.

Friendship cannot be inherited or transferred. It cannot be sealed and stowed away without rotting. Nor will it remain fresh forever in the deep freeze.

Friendship needs feeding. Some cultivate it with money while others with sweat or even blood. Friendship can be voracious, not to be satisfied with just the make-do. It feeds on time, the simplest yet most lavish nourishment of life. It requires sharing and listening with heart, looking each other in the eye when talking, and being all ears when listening. Friendship sometimes can be so brittle that it could be ruined by a mere unintended or misread remark, crumbling like a house under demolition. Friendship may also easily spoil, quickly turning sour because of an unproven hearsay. In a world of perpetual change and craving for the latest and newest, friendship is an exception. The ancient adage still holds true — friends are like antiques;

the older the better.

There are two kinds of gifts — practical and symbolic.

I like giving gifts of practical use, not only because they have functions that may serve a friend's immediate needs, but also out of a selfish consideration.

Those who are friends today may not necessarily be so a decade later.

Despite your steadfast loyalty, you might be altogether forgotten after all the years.

A practical and disposable gift, while being a current token of friendship, is also of value as food to the stomach or candy for the eye. It may also be something to make a friend smile or laugh or to be viewed with delight. I take comfort in knowing that although such gifts are disposable, they have brought moments of joy and beauty to friends. Gifts of symbolic value, on the other hand, will only be a source of embarrassment if they are kept when friendship is no more. My heart sinks, no matter how far away I may be, at knowing the sad fate of those keepsakes being either destroyed or discarded.

When it comes to gifts for oneself, the symbolic keepsakes are better. It could be a pebble or a leaf; plain looking to others, but of beauty and meaning decipherable only to you.

An address book is like a magic box from which you conjure up friends. I send S.O.S. to friends when I am in dire straits. The fear of loneliness lies in our subconsciousness like bugs in hibernation. The passing of time rewards you with friends as you go through life. I can be at times out of touch for days on end, yet safe in the knowledge of having already been spun into the web of enduring friendships.

Expediency is the greatest enemy of friendship as there is no such thing as lasting expediency. I cherish friends who have always been there for me through thick and thin. The camaraderie of the like-minded, each capable of touching the other's heart, is the stuff of legend, while alliances of expediency are short-lived. We put down our masks and open our heart to our friends; gloom and darkness become temporary and life is filled again with glorious light.

铁树一样的朋友

朋友这种宝贵的矿藏，不是白白得到的。

要得到最好的友情，首先要把自己当作最好的朋友，让自己觉得自己是被信任的，是被尊重的，然后你才会尊敬别人。

如果不尊重一个人，却想得到他的倾情相助，那不但是不可能，而且是不道德的。

我曾经很努力地照料一盆花，但那盆花还是死了。浇灌一盆花，尚且如此不易，照料一个朋友，当然也不是轻而易举的了。

朋友要处得长久，你一定要真性情。因为你若是假装，天长日久的，就太辛苦了。朋友也为难，因为他或她所喜爱的那个人，不是真正的你，而是一个伪装的你，这岂不是太荒谬？

当然，这种关系要求你的朋友也以真相示人，这样才能分辨大家是否真的投缘。如果彼此都真实并且喜欢，友情就牢固，经得起岁月淬火。如果彼此不能接受，那就友好地分手，互祝珍重。

要有时间听朋友唠叨，这几乎是一种时间的储蓄，因为你听他唠叨了，当你有这种需求的时候，他才有可能听你唠叨。听的时候要快，但反应的时候要三思而后行。

要有时间陪着朋友默默地走路，什么也不说，心却已然相知。

这样的朋友就像植物中的铁树，苍翠地绿着，很多年才开一次花。那花嫣然一笑，彼此都珍贵。

Friends Are like a Sago Palm

True friendships, precious like a gem, have to be earned.

For starters, you need to be your own best friend, trusting and respecting yourself for who you are, before you can accord others with the same.

It is not only impossible but also immoral to expect someone to be all out in helping you, if you don't even respect him.

I once tried hard in taking care of a potted plant but couldn't stop it from withering. If taking care of a potted plant is so hard, keeping a friend is even harder.

You have to open your heart and be your true self in a

friendship for it to last. You cannot pretend forever. It would be hard both for you and your friend. What a folly it would be if the one he or she likes were a fake; someone else in disguise!

Of course, such a relationship demands the other party to be genuine, too, so that both know it was written in the stars that they become true friends. If they genuinely like each other, their friendship will be solid and stand the test of time. Otherwise, it would be best to just throw in the towel and wish each other the best.

Invest in the time and lend a full ear to your friend when he just wants to talk. Being a good listener means you will likely be treated the same by your friend in your hour of need. Be quick to lend your ear, but think twice before you act.

Walk with your friend, even with nothing to be said. You touch his or her heart just by being there no matter what.

If you are such a friend, you will be like the sago palm; long-growing and ever green. Although rare and perhaps only once in many years, the showing of sago flowers is the most splendid and dearly cherished.

今世的五百次回眸

佛说，前世的五百次回眸，才换来今生的擦肩而过。顿生气馁，这辈子是没得指望了，和谁路遇和谁接踵，和谁相亲和谁反目，都是命定，挣扎不出。特别想到我今世从医，和无数病患咫尺对视。若干垂危之人，我手经治，每日查房问询，执腕把脉，相互间凝望的次数更是不可胜数，如有来世，将必定与他们相逢，是赖不脱躲不掉的。于是这一部分只有作罢，认了就是。但尚余一部分，却留了可以掌握的机缘。一些愿望，如果今生屡屡瞩目，就埋了一个下辈子擦肩而过的伏笔，待到日后便可再接再厉地追索和厮守。

今世，我将用余生五百次眺望高山。我始终认为高山是地球上最无遮掩的奇迹。一个浑圆的球，有不屈的坚硬的骨骼隆起，离太阳更近，离平原更远，它是这颗星球最勇敢最孤独的犄角。它经历了最残酷的折叠，也赢得了最高耸的荣誉。它有诞生也有消亡，它将被飓风抚平，它将被酸雨冲刷，它将把溃败的机体化作肥沃的土地，它将在柔和的平坦中温习伟大。我不喜欢任何关于征服高山的言论，以为那是人的菲薄和短视。真正的高山是不可能被征服的，它只是在某一个瞬间，宽容地接纳了登山者，让你在它头顶歇息片刻，给你一窥真颜的恩赐。如同一只鸟在树梢啼叫，它敢说自己把大树征服了吗？山的存在，让我们永葆谦逊和恭敬的姿态，知道在这个世界上，有一些事物必须仰视。

今生，我将用余生一千次不倦地凝望绿色。我少年戍边，有十年的时间面对的是皑皑冰雪，看到绿色的时间已经比他人少了许多。若是因为这份不属于我选择的怠慢，罚我下辈子少见绿色，岂不冤枉死了？记得在千百个与绿色隔绝的日子之后，我下了喀喇昆仑山，在新疆叶城突然看到辽阔的幽深绿色之后，第一反应竟是悚然，震惊中紧闭了双眼，如同看到密集的闪电。眼神荒疏了忘却了这人间最滋润的色彩，以为是虚妄的梦境。就在那一瞬，我皈依了绿色。这是最美丽的归宿，有了它，生命才得以繁衍和兴旺。常常听到说地球上的绿地到了××年末就全部沙化了，那是多么恐怖的期限。为了人类的长盛不衰，我以目光持久地祷告。

今生，我将用余生一万次目不转睛地注视人群。如果有来生，我期望还将成为他们中的一员，而不是其他的什么动物或是植物。尽管我知道人类有那么多可怕的弱点和缺陷，我还是为这个物种的智慧和勇敢而赞叹。我做过一次人类了，我知道了怎样才能更好地做人，做人是一门长久的功课，当我们刚刚学会了最初的运算，教科书就被合上。卷子才答了一半，收卷的铃声就响了，岂不遗憾？

把自己喜欢的事一一想来，我还要看海看花，看健美的运动员，看睿智的科学家，看慈祥的老人和欢快的少女，当然还有无邪的小童，突然就笑了。想我这余生，也不用干其他的事了，每天就在窗前屋后呆呆地看山看树看人群吧，以求个来世的擦肩而过。这样一路地看下去，来世的愿望不知能否得逞，今生的时光可就白白荒废了。于是决定，从此不再东张西望，只心定如水，把握当前。

不为虚渺的擦肩而过，而把余生定格在回眸之中。喜欢山所表达的精神，就游历和瞻仰山的峭拔和广博，期望自己也变得如此坚强。喜欢绿色和生命，喜爱人的丰饶和宝贵，就爱惜资源，尊重自己，也尊重他人。

Five Hundred Glances

The people we met in our lives were there for a reason —
they are the ones we had cast our glances at five hundred
times in our other lives, so the Buddha says. This, however,
discourages me. So we are all fated — whom to see and meet;
whom to love and hate. I was put in mind of my stint as a
medical professional, looking at patients in their multitudes,
each at close range. I had even pulled a number of them
back from the brink of death. The ones I had looked at as an
attending physician on ward rounds, holding their hands in
mine for pulse taking, with glances beyond numbering. If I
were to have some next life, I would see them all again with

no escaping. I guess I will just have to bite the bullet, for it is part of the deal. There is also a desirable part, one which you can control in a proactive way. What we desire, as long as we keep casting our glances at them in this life, will surely turn up in another for us to pursue and behold. It is like leaving a hint foreshadowing eventual encounters when the story moves to its premeditated end.

For the rest of my life, I will gaze upon towering mountains five hundred times. I have always thought mountains are earth's most visible wonders. The mountain ranges are the bulging bones of the otherwise round and smooth earth. Their towering peaks, pushed up by tremendous forces deep within, are closest to the sun, while the plains, far-flung and expansive, lie in earth's repose. They are rugged and stubborn, like the horns of a buffalo. Formed through brutal tectonic colliding and piling up of earth's crustal fragments, they rose to celebrated heights. Yet, their decline is almost simultaneous to their rise, as they are swept by winds and eroded by acid rains. Meanwhile, organic matters decompose to enrich soils.

Erosion produces softer contours that smooth over traces of great tectonic upheavals. I detest the brag about conquering high mountains, which says nothing but man's ill-advised arrogance and myopia. The mountains are unconquerable; they merely allow the climbers to bask momentarily in their magnanimity; for a reprieve at the peak and a peek at the sublime. How can a songbird, perching on a top twig and endlessly burbling, claim she has conquered the tree? Mountains teach us humility and reverence, reminding us that there are things in this world one must appreciate by looking up with a sense of awe.

For the rest of my life, I will train my gaze on all that is green a thousand times more. As a young soldier guarding a remote border post, I spent a decade facing nothing but snow and glaciers. That put me at a disadvantage when glances at green are tallied. It would be so unfair should such a lapse, not of my choosing, cause me to be punished in the next life with less green to see! I remember after thousands of days' not seeing any green, I descended from the mountain post in the Karakoram. My first sight of the vast expanse of deep green, upon reaching the oasis of Yecheng in Xinjiang, sent chills down my spine. I shut my eyes in shock as if being blinded by the sheer greenness — the rich, nourishing green, unfathomable like a mirage, which had hitherto been buried in oblivion. At that very moment, I became a convert. It was the most beautiful initiation. The green oasis is where life thrives. It is often said that the onslaught of desertification will eventually eat up all forests on earth in a certain number of years. What a horrifying prospect that is! I pray with a relenting gaze for humanity's evergreen future.

For the rest of my life, I will not turn my gaze away from the human multitudes. If there ever were to be the next life, I wish I will still be a member of the human race, rather than some other animal or plant. For all the woeful flaws, I applaud the wisdom and valour of the human species. Having been a human being once, I will have learned how to be a better person by next life. Yet the learning never ends. We wouldn't want to end up, do we, like an unwilling pupil who closes his textbook for good after having learned only the basic arithmetic, or finishes only half of his test when the school bells ring.

Come to think of it — I also want to fix my gaze at the ocean and wildflowers, athletes in their element and scientists at work, the kindly seniors and giggling girls, and of course the innocent toddlers. I chuckle at my movable list and the thought that I could very well spend the rest of my life doing nothing but staring — at mountains, trees, and people old and young. I have no way to be certain what all this gazing for the sake of next life will come to. What is certain is the rest of my life would thus be squandered. Therefore, I resolve to pull myself together, seize the moment and live in the present, not to keep throwing glances east and west.

So we will not be spending the rest of our lives doing nothing but glancing around, merely for the sake of uncertain encounters in our next lives. Go to the mountains and admire their immensity and majestic precipices, if you feel they are calling. Their rugged power will flow into you and make you strong. Take care of the environment and respect yourself and others, if you cherish the lush green of forests, the vigour of life, and the great diversity of humanity.

流露你的真表情

学医的时候，先生问过一道题，人和动物在解剖形态上的最大区别是什么？

当学生的争先恐后地发言，都想由自己说出那个正确的答案。这看起来并不是个很难的问题。

有人说，是站立行走。先生说，不对。大猩猩也是可以站立的。

有人说，是懂得用火。先生不悦道，我问的是生理上的区别，并不是进化上的。

更有同学答，是劳动创造了人。先生说，你在社会学上也许可以得满分，但请听清我的问题。

满室寂然。

先生见我们混沌不悟，自答道，记住，是表情啊。地球上没有任何一科生物有人类这样丰富的表情肌。比如笑吧，一只狗再聪明也是不会笑的。人类的近亲猴子勉强算作会笑，但只能做出龇牙咧嘴一种表情。只有人类，才可以调动面部的所有肌群，调整出不同的笑容，比如微笑，比如嘲笑，比如冷笑，比如狂笑，以表达自身复杂的情感。我在惊讶中记住了先生的话，以为是至理名言。

近些年来，我开始怀疑先生教了我一条谬误。

乘坐飞机，起飞之前，每次都有空姐为我们演示一遍空中遭遇紧急情形时，如何打开氧气面罩的操作。我乘坐飞机数十次，每一次都凝神细察，但从未看清过具体步骤。空姐满面笑容地屹立前舱，脸上很真诚，手上却很敷衍，好像在做一种太极功夫，点到为止，全然顾及不到这种急救措施对乘客是怎样的性命攸关。我分明看到了她们脸上悬挂的笑容和冷淡的心的分离，升起一种被愚弄的感觉。

我有一位相识许久的女友，原是个敢怒敢恨、敢涕泪滂沱敢笑逐颜开的性情中人。几年不见，不知在哪里读了淑女规范言行的著作，同我谈话的时候身子仄仄地欠着，双膝款款地屈着，嘴角勾勒成一个精致的角度。粗一看，你以为她时时在微笑，细一看，你就捉摸不透她的真表情，心里不禁有些发毛。你若在背后叫她，她是不会立刻回了头来看你，而是端端地将身体转了过来，从容地瞄着你，说骤然回头会使脖子上的肌肤提前衰老。

她是那样吝啬使用她的表情，虽然她给你一个温馨的外表，却没有丝毫的温度。我看着她，不由得想起儿时戴的大头娃娃面具。

遇到过一位哭哭啼啼的饭店服务员，说她一切按店方的要求去办，不想却被客人责难。那客人匆忙之中丢失了公文包，要她帮助寻找。客人焦急地述说着，她耐心地倾听着，正思谋着如何帮忙，客人竟勃然大怒了，吼着说，我急得火烧眉毛，你竟然还在笑。你是在嘲笑我吗？

我那一刻绝没有笑。服务员指天咒地对我说。

看她的眼神，我相信是真话。

那么，你当时做了怎样一个表情呢？我问，恍恍惚惚探到了一点头绪。

喏，我就是这样的……她侧过脸，把那刻的表情模拟给我。

那是一个职业女性训练有素的程式化的表情，

眉梢扬着，嘴角翘着……

无论我多么同情她，我还是要说，这是一张空洞漠然的笑脸。

服务员的脸，已经被长期的工作塑造成她自己也不能控制的状态。

表情肌不再表达人类的感情了，或者说它们只表达一种感情，那就是微笑。

我们的生活中曾经排斥微笑，关于那个时代我们已经做了结论。于是我们呼吁微笑、引进微笑、培育微笑，微笑就泛滥起来。荧屏上著名和不著名的男女主持人无时无刻不在微笑，以至于使人不得不产生疑问，我们的生活中真有那么多值得微笑的事情吗？

微笑变得越来越商业化了。他对你微笑，并不表明他的善意，微笑只是金钱的等价物。他对你微笑，并不表明他的诚恳，微笑只是恶战的前奏。他对你微笑，并不说明他想帮助你，微笑只是一种谋略。他对你微笑，并不证明他对你的友谊，微笑只是麻痹你的一重帐幕……

这样的事见得太多之后，竟对微笑的本质怀疑起来。

亿万年的进化，我们的身体本身就成了一本书。

人的眉毛为什么要如此飞扬，轻松地直抵鬓角？那是因为此刻为鏖战的间隙，我们不必紧皱眉头思考，精神得以豁然舒展。

人的上眼睑肌为什么要如此松弛，使眼裂缩小，眼神迷离，目光不再聚焦？那是因为面对朋友，可以放松警惕敞开心扉，放松自己紧张的神经，不必目光炯炯。

人的嘴角为什么上挑，不再抿成森然一线？那是因为随时准备开启双唇，倾吐热情的话语，饮下甘甜的琼浆。

因为快乐和友情，从猿到人，演变出了美妙动人的微笑，这是人类无与伦比的财富。笑容像一只模型，把我们脸上的肌肉像羊群一般驯化了，让它们按照微笑的规则排列，随时以备我们心情的调遣。

假若不是服从心情的安排，只是表情肌机械的动作，那无异于噩梦中抽筋，除了遗留久久的酸痛，与快乐是毫无关联的。

记得小时候读过大文豪雨果的《笑面人》，一个苦孩子被施了刑法，脸被固定成狂笑的模样。他痛苦不堪，因为他的任何表情，都只能使脸上狂笑的表情更为惨烈。

无时无刻不在笑——这是一种刑罚，它使"笑"这种人类最美丽最优美的表情，蜕化为一种酷刑。

现代自然没有这种刑罚了。但如果不表达自己的心愿，只是一味地微笑着，微笑像画皮一样黏附在我们的脸庞上，像破旧的门帘沉重地垂着，完全失掉了真诚善良的原始含义，那岂不是人类进化的大退步、大哀痛？

人类的表情肌除了表达笑容，还用以表达愤怒、悲哀、思索、惆怅以至绝望。它就像天空中的七色彩虹，相辅相成，所有的表情都是完整的人生所必需的，是生命的元素。

我们既然具备了流泪的本能，哀伤的时候就该听凭那些满含盐分的浊水淌出体外。血脉贲张、目眦俱裂，不论是为红颜还是为功名，未必不是人生的大境界。额头没有一丝皱纹的美人，只怕血管里流动的都是冰。表情是心情的档案，如果永远只是空白，谁还愿把最重要的记录留在上面？

当然，我绝不是主张人人横眉冷对。经过漫长的隧道，我们终于笑起来了，这是一个大进步，但笑也是分阶段，也是有层次的。空洞而浅薄的笑如同盲目的恨和无缘无故的悲哀一样，都是情感的赝品。

有一句话叫作"笑比哭好"，我常常怀疑它。笑和哭都是人类的正常情绪反应，谁能说黛玉临终时的笑比哭好呢？

痛则大悲，喜则大笑，只要是从心底流出的对世界的真情感，都是生命之壁的摩崖石刻，经得起岁月风雨的打磨，值得我们久久珍爱。

Just Be Yourself and Let Them Know it

When I was in medical school, our teacher had once raised a question: "What is the biggest difference between humans and animals as far as biological features are concerned?"

We students rushed to be first in giving the right answer, considering the question as quite easy.

One said: "It is walking in an upright position!"

The teacher retorted: "No. The ape can move upright just as well."

Another said: "It is the use of fire." The teacher reminded the class: "I am talking about biological differences, not in terms of evolution."

And then another: "It is the theory about man being created by labour." The teacher retorted: "You will get a good grade in a sociology course, but you should listen carefully to my question."

The room fell silent.

Seeing how dense we were, the teacher answered his own question. "Remember this," he said, "it is facial expression. There is no other species on earth which has as many facial expressions as the human race. Take laughing for instance. A dog, however smart, cannot laugh. At a pinch, you could say that the monkey, closest to the human race, can laugh. But it is just a grimace, showing its teeth. It is the human race, and the human race only, that can control all the muscles on his or her face and show different kinds of expressions, such as the smile, or a look of derision, or a stare of contempt, or the guffaw etc that expresses one's different feelings." The teacher's words gave me a shock and I always remembered them as the ultimate truth.

But as Time went by, I had second thoughts and began to suspect that the teacher may have fed me a big lie.

Take flying, for example. Before take-off, the air hostess would regularly make a demonstration of how to deal with a crisis, such as putting on a oxygen mask and so on. I had flown dozens of times and had always listened to those instructions, but was never given a chance to see them put into practice. The air hostesses would stand in a row in the front cabin, looking very eager but with their hands listlessly moving about, as if they were practicing tai chi, totally unconcerned about what they were doing. The smiles hanging on their faces were totally devoid of any consciousness that this was a matter of life and death as far as the travellers were concerned. The detachment between the smile hanging on the lips of these young women and the cold in their hearts was so obvious. I felt that I had been made a fool of.

I have a longstanding girl friend of many years. Quite a character, she used to be. She would let herself go, flying into a temper or splitting her sides with laughter, as her mood decided. We had been out of touch for a couple of years.

Who knows where and when she had gotten herself hooked on a book about young women's social behaviour! Nowadays, speaking to me, her body would be slightly slanted towards me while her knees were slightly bent. Her lips were touched up into a curve which formed a permanent smile, though on a closer look you are not sure what was she trying to express, and somehow you get rattled. If you called her from behind, do not expect her to respond immediately. Holding her body upright, she will turn around slowly. Then, looking at you placidly, she will tell you that turning around too precipitately will coarsen the skin on one's neck.

She was so niggardly in expression that even though she carries herself off as a warm-hearted person, there was not the slightest warmth emanating from her. As I looked at her, I was reminded of the huge toy masks that we children used to put on for fun.

Then I met a tearful waitress at a hotel. She said she had done everything according to order, but was still scolded by a guest. The fact was that the guest had lost his briefcase and had asked the waitress to look for it. She listened meekly as the guest gave his instructions, musing on how to go about looking for the briefcase when suddenly the guest broke out passionately: "I am dying of anxiety, and you dare to laugh! Are you laughing at me?"

"Certainly not, sir!" The waitress snapped as she appealed to me.

Looking at her in the eye, I believed her.

"What did you do to provoke him?" I asked, trying to make sense of the whole business.

"Oh, all I did was this ... " She turned sideways and repeated her former expression. It was the typical facial expression of professional women at the time ... eyebrows raised, lips pouting.

Now I must acknowledge that no matter how much I sympathize with the waitress, I must still say that hers was a face with a vacuous expression.

The fact was, the face of the waitress had been shaped by constant practice and moulded beyond her own control.

The muscles controlling her expression, no longer express human feelings, or rather, they were limited to one kind of expression only — the smile.

There had been a time in the past, when the smile had been banished. By now, however, we have passed judgment on that era and demand the return of the smile. We import the smile, we nourish the smile, and the smile ran amok. Famous and not so famous anchor men and anchor women are smiling non-stop, making us ask ourselves: Are there so many things in our life that call for a smile?

The smile has become increasingly commercialized.

He smiles at you but it does not mean that he is well-intentioned towards you — the smile is merely the equivalent of its value in hard cash,

He smiles at you but it does not mean that he is earnest — the smile is a means to disarm you ahead of the coming battle,

He smiles at you, but that does not mean that he is willing to help you — it is just a ploy,

He smiles at you, but that is not a sign of his friendship — he is using a curtain to misinform you.

Having encountered so many such smiles, one starts to question the nature of the smile.

Having gone through eons of evolution, our body is a book in itself.

Now why should our eyebrows turn upwards, easily reaching our brows? Because the present is a lull in the strife of life, we can afford to loosen up a bit and give ourselves a break!

Now why is it that our eyebrows are loose, minimizing the space between our eyelids, causing our line of vision to be scattered? Being among friends, our line of vision need not be so concentrated. We can relax and enjoy ourselves without having to shoot our line of vision in every direction.

Now why do our lips turn upwards making a curve instead of a straight line? — So that we can open our mouths at any time and carry on intimate conversations, or enjoy a flavoured drink!

Thanks to happiness and friendship, from ape to man the human smile evolved, beautiful and moving, an imitable human legacy. The smiling face is like a model, modifying the flesh on our faces as if they were a bunch of sheep, filed according to their smiles, ready to reach out to us at all times, ready to go at an order from our heart.`

If not bending to an impulse from the heart, if merely limited to a mechanical play of the nerves, laughter would just be a spasm in a nightmare, having nothing to do with pleasure and enjoyment.

I remember reading *The Man who Laughs* by Victor Hugo, about a poor boy who was branded so that his face was a permanent grimace. Any other facial expression that he attempts would only exacerbate the horror.

To be laughing at all times — it is a torture. It would make laughter — mankind's most beautiful expression — disintegrate into a form of torture.

Nowadays, of course, there are no more such forms of torture.

But if we do not make a stand but just keep smiling, then the "laughter," like a piece of "painted skin" stuck to our face, like a discarded piece of door hanging, will lose its original spirit of upholding honesty and kindness, and that will mean a big step backwards for the human race, a great tragedy.

The tools of expression of the human race, apart from expressing laughter, is also used to express anger, sorrow, thought, confusion and even despair.

It is like the colours of the rainbow in the sky, contrasting and coordinating with each other, forming the essence of life.

Since we are gifted with the ability to cry, then we should let the salty water drip freely down our cheeks when we are sad. And then to be hot-blooded and to rage, be it for love or glory, is by no means all ignoble. Those aloof beauties without a wrinkle on their forehead could well be cold of heart. Expressions reflect our emotions and a blank look reflects a barren heart.

Of course, I am not for fervent animosity. After an era of acrimony among fellow men, we have learned to greet each other with smiles again, which is remarkable progress. Yet there is also an aspect of quality to smiling. That which is frivolous is but spurious and unauthentic, no different from blind hatred and senseless sorrow.

It is said that smiling is better than crying, which I rather doubt. To me, both are natural emotional responses. Who can say that Lin Daiyu's deathbed smile (in *Dream of the Red Chamber*) is better than crying?

Grieve when in deep pain; laugh when in joy. Heart-felt emotions are sparks of life to be cherished; indelible like engravings in a stone cliff that can bear up the erosive power of time and the elements.

你还能找到北斗吗

有一天，走进一间大大的办公室。它有多大呢？简直像个足球场。一排排的格子，好像非洲白蚁的巢穴。每个小格子里都有一台电脑，几乎所有的电脑都开着，一眼望去，仿佛一片片闪着不同光泽的鳞甲，颤抖着，忽闪着。突然好奇，我对大家说，我想看看你们的桌面。

这个桌面不是木头的桌面，而是计算机的屏幕。

微软公司配发的桌面，是一片绿色的原野，芳草茵茵，略有坡度和起伏，有如少女肩胛一般柔和的地平线，还有蓝天和白云。

这是哪里？恕我孤陋寡闻，我不知道。那一年到了冰岛，极目远眺，绿水青山，觉得有些像，然而，终不是。

据说，人类是发源于东非高原。那里水草丰美，有蜿蜒的河流，稀疏的林木，宽广的空间……想想那时人类的生存状况，能理解他们的选择。必要有流水，否则，在没有打井和储水设备的时候，谁来保障水的供给？只有河。

需要相对的开阔。早期的人类和凶猛的野兽比较起来，势单力孤。如果居所在密林中，真有什么野兽无声无息地接近营地，将是非常危险的局面。

要有林木。如果危险的对手不会爬树，从大猩猩进化来的古人类，攀缘的本领一定还不错，必要时爬到树上，或可躲过一劫。

不知他们那时，是否已经学会了刀耕火种？开阔的地形上，也许可以开点小片荒地，种瓜种豆，聊补生计。

扯得远了，回到咱们的正题。

我觉得微软的这屏桌面实在是很妙，它是远古人类生存环境的再现，看到它的时候，每一个细胞的记忆都被调动，人会情不自禁地安静下来，涌起稳定的愉悦。

不过，再好的东西，终日享受也有厌倦的时候。人是喜新厌旧的动物，这不是缺点，只是弱点。于是人们就各显其能，换上了个性化的桌面。感谢大家，让我在同一个时间内看到了丰富多彩的屏幕桌面。

后来，我就像有窥视癖的心理变态者一样，经常不动声色地悄悄端详别人的电脑。好在大家对电脑中的内容保密警惕性很高，但对桌面屏幕却采取了大大咧咧、任由参观的态度。

屏幕上什么景色最多？猜一猜。

大多数人都能猜对。屏幕上出现最多的景色是大自然，尤以绿色为多。草地或是森林，还有盛开的天真烂漫的花。

其次是海洋和蓝天。蓝得令人想下跪的大海，翻卷的浪花如羊群一般柔美。朝霞或晚霞，瑰丽如火。

还有很多蝴蝶、禽鸟、热带鱼的图片。

我本来以为会有人物图片，比如恋人啊，孩子啊。有一些，比例不高。还有一点，让人比较吃惊。把自己父母图片当作屏幕的，一个也没有（也许，一打开电脑，就看见父母殷切目光，实在是个压力。躲了吧）。

小小统计之后，我想说，人们是多么渴望在大自然当中遨游啊。

可是，这个简单的期望，并不容易满足。不信，你问问自己，你有多少天没有仰望星空？还能找到北斗七星的位置吗？你有多少天没有到公园中玩耍，看到盛开的花朵，闻到芬芳了？你有多少天没有听到纯净的流水声，也就是干净的大海和深山的小溪发出的声响？

很多人都会说，很久了很久了。

把电脑屏幕上的大自然换成真的风景吧，迈开你的双腿！

Can You Find the Plough?

One day, I walked into an enormous open-plan office. How large is it? It is almost the size of a football field, with row upon row of cubicles, dense as an African ant colony. In each cubicle, a computer monitor flickered like the shimmering scale of some gigantic fish. I was seized by an urge to know more and said, "May I take a look at your desktop?"

I meant the home screen of their computers, of course, not the wooden top of their desks.

The default Windows Vista desktop then was a photographic image of rolling green hills, with a soft contour line, like that of a girl's sloping shoulder, and a blue sky with swirls of white clouds.

Where was this photograph taken? Forgive me for my ignorance; I have no clue. I visited Iceland that year and did find the green hills there reaching far into the horizon looked similar. But those were not the source of Windows image for sure.

The earliest humans are said to have come from the highlands of East Africa. The open savannas and lush grasslands, in a region with serpentine rivers running through it, are indeed life-giving. Given the conditions of their existence then, we can understand the choice of the early humans to settle there. There must be water. When the early humans had no means to dig wells or store water, rivers and streams were their only sources.

There must also be clearings. The early humans were no match to ferocious carnivores. Thick, closed forests would allow predators to sneak up on a camp, putting human survival in peril.

Then there must also be trees. If the predators could not

climb trees, the early humans had a better chance to escape by getting up the tree. They should all had good climbing skills, as they shared last common ancestors with chimpanzees.

I digressed. Let's return to the subject at hand.

To me, Microsoft's Windows Vista desktop looked quite amazing. It was an image that harkens back to humanity's idyllic, pastoral past. When we gazed at it, something deep in our consciousness was stoked. We became peaceful, with a serene sense of bliss welling up inside us.

However, we may still be bored with even an image of bliss, after staring at it all day however great it may be. Humans are novelty seekers, which, though not a crime, is a weakness. People would experiment and switch to various customized desktops. I am thankful for all that ingenuity which allowed me to see a multitude of desktops all at once.

Then I became something of a voyeur, getting accustomed to peering at other people's computer screens, often surreptitiously. Luckily, everyone was vigilant enough when it comes to protecting what is on their computer, but relaxed and cool with their desktop, not averse to an inadvertent glance by another.

So what is the most popular image people use for their desktop?

Most would have guessed it right: scenes of nature, predominantly green — meadows, forests and flowers in riotous blossom — are top of the list.

Next on the list are ocean and sky; a sky bluer than blue and ocean with foaming white breakers that take on the fluffiness of fleece. The sunrise and sunset paint the sky with fiery swirls of pink.

Then there were also images of butterflies, birds and tropical fish.

I had thought I would see images of people, too; loved ones and children, for example. There were some of these, which represent only a small proportion. Then I noted something amiss with a shock: there were no images of one's parents. Not on a single desktop. (Perhaps seeing the earnest gaze of one's elder every time the computer is turned on is just too much to bear. People choose to hide.)

My little survey showed that there is so much yearning to be immersed in nature, so I concluded.

Yet this simple desire of ours is not so easy to satisfy. If you don't agree, you should ask yourself, "When was the last time I gazed at a sky full of stars?" Can you still find the Plough and the North Star? How long ago did you last play in a park, see flowers in full blossom and sniff their sweet scents? When did you last hear the singing of pure water — the gurgling of streams in the mountains and the lapping of crystalline ocean waves at the shore?

Many would agree it was ages ago.

Then turn away from the vista of your computer. Get out into nature. Hit the trail!